305.80
THO

3-20.96	DATE DUE		
APR 22 1997			
MAY 12 1997			
FE 17 '00			
MR 01 '00			
MR 16 '00			
FE 26 '01			
MR 26 '01			
MY 07 '01			

Hate Groups

Look for these and other books in the Lucent
Overview series:

Abortion
Acid Rain
AIDS
Alcoholism
Animal Rights
The Beginning of Writing
Cancer
The Collapse of the Soviet Union
Dealing with Death
Death Penalty
Democracy
Drugs and Sports
Drug Trafficking
Eating Disorders
Endangered Species
Energy Alternatives
Espionage
Extraterrestrial Life
Gangs
Garbage
The Greenhouse Effect
Gun Control
Hate Groups
Hazardous Waste

The Holocaust
Homeless Children
Illiteracy
Immigration
Ocean Pollution
Oil Spills
The Olympic Games
Organ Transplants
Ozone
Population
Prisons
Rainforests
Recycling
The Reunification of Germany
Smoking
Space Exploration
Special Effects in the Movies
Teen Alcoholism
Teen Pregnancy
Teen Suicide
The UFO Challenge
The United Nations
Vietnam

Hate Groups

by Sharon Elaine Thompson

LUCENT
B·O·O·K·S

LUCENT Overview Series

Blairsville High School Library

Library of Congress Cataloging-in-Publication Data

Thompson, Sharon Elaine, 1952-
    Hate groups / by Sharon Elaine Thompson.
        p.   cm. — (Overview series)
    Includes bibliographical references and index.
    Summary: Presents an overview of those groups, past and present,
formed to promote the hatred of and violence against targeted
minorities and explores ways to foster understanding and peaceful
coexistence.
    ISBN 1-56006-144-8 (acid-free paper)
    1. Racism—United States. 2. Violence—United States. 3. United
States—Race relations. 4. Freedom of speech—United States.
[1. White supremacy movements. 2. Racism. 3. Race relations.
4. Freedom of speech.] I. Title. II. Series: Lucent overview
series.
E184.A1T53   1994
305.8'00973—dc20   93-19107
                                                        CIP
                                                         AC

No part of this book may be reproduced or used in any form or by any means, electrical,
mechanical, or otherwise, including, but not limited to, photocopy, recording, or any
information storage and retrieval system, without prior written permission from the publisher.

Copyright © 1994 by Lucent Books, Inc.
P.O. Box 289011, San Diego, CA 92198-9011
Printed in the U.S.A.

For Patrick Charles Walsh (1969-1989)
who was killed shortly before his twentieth birthday,
a victim of racial hatred.
And for his mother, Linda Gugler Walsh,
who helps other victims of crime
and guarantees that Patrick, although a victim,
will never become a statistic.

Contents

Introduction

"WHOM THEY FEAR they hate," wrote Roman poet Quintus Ennius two hundred years before the birth of Christ. Two thousand years later, fear is still the root of hatred.

A person may fear another person for many different reasons. Individuals may be afraid of someone who has threatened them or done them harm. They may also fear persons, such as those who commit crimes, who have the potential to do them harm.

However, individuals may also fear someone who has not hurt them at all—perhaps someone they do not know, but whose appearance or background differs from their own. Judging a person strictly on appearance or background is called prejudice. Prejudice arises most often in connection with race, religion, ethnic background, or sexual orientation. In most cases, prejudice is based on ignorance.

Prejudiced people may try to control or hide their fear and ignorance by making themselves feel superior, or better than, the person they fear. One way prejudiced people make themselves feel superior is by name calling. Many ugly names have been uttered over the years by people striking at those they fear and do not know.

A demeaning name or label directed at one person sometimes targets an entire group of peo-

(Opposite page) American Nazis march in Chicago, Illinois. Nazi beliefs caught fire during a period of deep frustration in Germany in the 1920s and 1930s.

ple. When this happens, the name-caller ceases to view members of that group as individuals. If one member of a group looks or acts a certain way, prejudiced people assume that *all* members of the group will be the same.

Fueling prejudice

Making broad judgments about everyone in a group based on the actions or characteristics of one person is called stereotyping. Stereotypes can be based on positive characteristics: all soldiers are brave, for example. But most often, people stereotype others with negative traits. Usually groups of people are stereotyped with negative labels such as dirty, stupid, or thieving. Negative stereotypes fuel prejudice and, in some ways, heighten fear.

Uncontrollable events such as the loss of a home or job can also breed fear, especially when they are the result of wide-scale economic or social change. Because people can do little to control this sort of change, they sometimes react with anger and frustration. When people are frightened and angry, they often look for someone or something to blame. If there is no one or nothing specific to blame, that person may look for a scapegoat—any person or group who *can* be blamed. The scapegoat is rarely someone we know and almost always someone who is different from ourselves in some way.

People who share fears, prejudices, and a need for quick solutions and easy targets sometimes join together in a hate group. Hate group members find comfort in uniting against people of a different race, religion, ethnic background, or sexual orientation. Hate groups can form anywhere in the world where different peoples come into contact. In the United States and Europe today, the term hate group commonly refers to

The Ku Klux Klan brings its hateful message to a 1990 rally in Houston, Texas.

Reprinted by permission of Clay Bennet and the *St. Petersburg Times.*

white supremacists, people who belong to the white race and who consider themselves superior to anyone who is not white. Most white supremacists today also target those who are not Protestant Christians—particularly Jews.

In recent years, the membership in North American and European hate groups has begun to grow. Hate groups are finding new members among those who are frightened by rising unemployment, waves of immigration, and by social change. Hate groups are responsible for a growing number of crimes against minorities. Random hate crimes by individuals who do not belong to an organized group are also on the rise.

The actions of hate groups are often ignored by those who are not affected directly. If hate groups are ignored too long, their evil may grow. Edmund Burke, a member of the British Parliament, recognized this potential problem as early as the 1700s. Historians believe he said, "The only thing necessary for the triumph of evil is for good men to do nothing."

Only tolerant people of all backgrounds can stop the hate. Many people have already begun this work. However, much more work lies ahead.

1

The Rise of Hate Groups

FEAR, ANGER, FRUSTRATION, and igno-
rance are the roots of hatred. These feelings exist
to some degree in almost any population, but they
strengthen in times of economic hardship, large-
scale immigration, and massive social change.
This is because these conditions often bring huge
and confusing changes to people's lives, which in
turn spark fear. Frightened people sometimes
look for scapegoats on which to blame their fears.
Within this unstable atmosphere, hate groups
grow. By looking at some of the hate groups that
have developed over the past 150 years, it is possible to see the contribution of sweeping economic and social changes on the rise of such
groups.

Immigration and the Know-Nothings

One of the first organizations in the United
States that could be called a hate group was the
Order of the Star-Spangled Banner. It was
founded in New York City in 1849. Because
members wanted to keep the group secret, they
were supposed to say, "I know nothing," when
asked about their organization. Thus the group
was called the Know-Nothings.

*(Opposite page) White robed Ku
Klux Klan members march in
1925 down Pennsylvania
Avenue in Washington, D.C. In
terms of numbers, the KKK
reached its height in the 1920s.*

The group formed at a time of massive economic and social change in the United States. Rapidly expanding railroads and the rise of factories disrupted traditional small-town life. Towns bypassed by the rails withered and died as businesses closed and young people moved away to cities where work was plentiful.

Americans saw their way of life changing. They were aware that the railroads and factories were somehow to blame for the changes, but they could not take their anger out on these institutions. Instead, many found a scapegoat in the more than 3 million foreigners who arrived in the United States seeking land and work between 1846 and 1855. Many of these immigrants had been driven from Europe by famine, war, and land shortages. About half of them were Irish Catholics.

Because many of the new immigrants found jobs with the railroads and in the factories, displaced Americans blamed the foreigners for unemployment and the changing patterns of work and family life. They also accused the newcomers of increasing the number of slums and of "violations of the sabbath, drunkenness, pauperism, brawling and crime," according to Yale University historian Michael Holt.

Targets of anger

The main targets of the Know-Nothings' anger were Roman Catholic immigrants—primarily Irish Catholics. The Know-Nothings, or nativists as they were sometimes called because they favored native-born Americans over new immigrants, considered Catholicism a foreign and undesirable religion. Most Americans at the time were Protestants and knew little about Catholicism. So when the Know-Nothings spread rumors about a Catholic plot to overthrow the government or massacre all Protestants, their words

Immigrants seeking new lives in the United States in the 1800s were an easy target for American prejudice and hatred.

"helped foment an almost hysterical fear and antagonism to Catholics," writes Holt. Hysteria rose even in towns where there were no Catholics or immigrants. As one observer wrote, "Nearly everybody appears to have gone altogether deranged [crazy] on Nativism here."

The Know-Nothings attacked Irish Catholics, stoned their homes, and burned their churches. On election day, armed vigilantes—citizens who organize to punish crime and enforce the law as they see fit—roamed sections of the cities where immigrants lived to prevent the new citizens from voting. The nativists feared that once the immigrants became citizens, they would be elected to public office and pass laws that favored the immigrants.

Despite their views and behavior the Know-Nothings would not have considered themselves a hate group. They believed their way of life and even their government were threatened by for-

Members of the Pennsylvania militia battle a mob of rioting Know-Nothings in 1844 in Philadelphia.

eigners, and that they were "defending American institutions from a terrible menace," writes Holt. Through force, secrecy, and laws that would protect the native-born, Holt says, the Know-Nothings thought they could "impose order and control on their changing society."

The Know-Nothings reached their peak in 1855. Interest in their cause declined after that, as American attention shifted from immigrants to the issue of abolishing slavery and, later, the Civil War.

Bitterness in the South

The bitter struggle between the industrial North and the agricultural South ended slavery in the United States. But it also ended a way of life for white Southerners. The Southern states' economies had been based on large plantations of cotton and tobacco and on the slave labor that allowed them to produce those crops. Without slaves to work the fields, plantation owners could not produce their crops. Without crops, there

A group of freed slaves poses for a photograph shortly after the Civil War. Southerners bitter in the aftermath of the Civil War vented their anger on freed black slaves.

were no earnings. People starved and businesses went bankrupt.

In addition, the federal government sent representatives from the North to run Southern state governments. Southerners distrusted the Northerners and resented outsiders from the North telling them how to run their state governments.

The loss of their way of life, the presence of a Northern military government, the grinding postwar poverty, and the federal government's insistence that blacks be treated equally with whites angered and frustrated white Southerners. They could not strike back against the government in Washington, which they felt was responsible for their losses. But they *could* strike back at the black people who had worked as their slaves. During this time of deep anger and frustration, the Ku Klux Klan (KKK) was born.

Nightriders in bedsheets

Historians believe that six ex-Confederate soldiers started the Ku Klux Klan. Dressing up in bedsheets and masks, they rode after dark through the town of Pulaski, Tennessee, frightening black ex-slaves. Their behavior turned uglier as the economic depression in the South continued. Membership in the Klan grew and their activities became more violent. Robed and hooded Klan members shot up houses and dragged people from their beds to tar-and-feather or beat them. Some victims were killed.

When federal troops withdrew from the South in 1877, white Southerners regained control over their states governments. Their anger and frustration lessened. Membership in the Klan declined as a result.

But the Klan did not die. Over the past 130 years, in response to changes in society, the Klan has periodically reappeared.

It first reappeared in the 1920s. The 1920s marked another period of change in American society. The role of women was the focus of much of this change. Drinking, smoking, and dancing had once been considered unbecoming behavior for a woman. But many women decided they enjoyed these and other activities that had long been forbidden to them. Many women adopted the flashy dress and behavior of the period, rejecting the modest lifestyle previously open to them.

Some of the people who were most troubled by these and other changes turned to the Klan. The Klan promised a "crusade for old-time fundamentalist religion, clean living, 100 percent Americanism, and law and order. Invocations of God, flag, and country, more than of white supremacy, spurred [the Klan's] spectacular success," writes Richard Tucker, author of *The Dragon and the Cross*. Many churches rallied behind the Klan. As

A Ku Klux Klan march in 1924 in Binghampton, New York. The Klan attracted thousands of members in the 1920s with talk of a return to "clean living" and "old-time fundamentalist religion."

many as forty thousand ministers joined, and Klan members regularly addressed church congregations. People joined by the thousands. Most of the new members were from the Midwest. By the late 1920s, Klan officials claimed that 4 million of America's 113 million citizens had joined their organization.

The midwestern Klan members campaigned against bootleggers, speakeasies, immoral books and movies, and nightclubs. But the Klan targeted even more. According to Patsy Sims, author of *The Klan*, their victims included "anyone, anything, the Klan didn't like, and its dislikes were many: Negroes, Jews, Catholics, Orientals, Mormons, immigrants. . . ."

Of these groups, the Klan's primary targets were Catholics. To fuel anti-Catholic feelings, the KKK spread rumors that women were tortured in convents, that Catholics stored arms in church basements, and that the bodies of infants fathered

The restrained behavior of the past fell away in the 1920s, as American women freely experimented with flashy dress, public drinking, dancing, and smoking.

The Ku Klux Klan's national leader, Hiram Evans, takes part in a Klan rally in 1926. Evans once said that Jews and Catholics were a "menace to Americanism."

by priests were buried under convents. On one occasion the Klan's national leader, Imperial Wizard Hiram Evans, stated the Klan's position: Jews and Roman Catholics were a "menace to Americanism."

In the late 1920s, newspapers began to publish stories about the Klan's role in political corruption and bribery, and about the questionable behavior of one of its leaders. This conflicted with the Klan's claim that it supported law and order and Christian morality. Thousands of Americans, disgusted by the Klan and the behavior of its members, cancelled their memberships.

Challenges to segregation

By the 1940s, the Klan had largely disappeared again, but only temporarily. On May 17, 1954, the U.S. Supreme Court ordered the desegregation, or a halt to racial separation, of American public schools. In reaction, the Klan reappeared, proclaiming a message of white supremacy.

Until the 1950s, many Southern states had laws supporting racial segregation or separation. By law, black and white students attended different schools. Black and white Southerners ate in different restaurants, sat separately on buses, swam in different public pools, and even drank from separate water fountains.

The Supreme Court ruling directly affected only the schools. But other challenges to segregation followed, and many white Southerners felt threatened by the changes occurring in their lives. They believed that desegregation would ruin schools and their children's education and that educated African-Americans would compete with them for jobs. They had lost control, they feared, of their children's future and their own.

As it had in the past, the sense of fear and unease created an opening for the Klan. Southerners rallied in support of the policy stated three decades earlier by Klan chaplain Caleb Ridley: "The first principle of the Klan is that it is a white man's organization. . . . The Klan believes in the supremacy of the Anglo-Saxon race, now and forever. This is a white man's country. . . ."

Klan membership grew rapidly and Klan activities once again became violent. Between 1956 and 1966 the Klan committed more than a thousand acts of terror, beating, acid throwing, and murder against black citizens and black and white civil rights workers, primarily in the South.

Court-ordered school desegregation challenged color barriers, especially in the South. In 1957, Elizabeth Eckford (center front) bravely walks past National Guardsmen and shouting students in an effort to enroll at Central High School in Little Rock, Arkansas.

Klan membership rose to 42,000 in 1965. But the general public was appalled by the Klan's violent behavior and hateful views. Public disapproval, strong police enforcement, prosecution by the U.S. Justice Department, and juries who were not afraid to convict Klan members put the Klan out of business. By 1974 membership was down to 1,500. Although its nationwide membership climbed to 5,000 members during the 1980s and 1990s, the Klan has never regained its former status.

The Know-Nothings and the Ku Klux Klan waged most of their wars on American soil. This has not been the case with all hate groups. Germany was the cradle of possibly the most notor-

Klan membership has risen and fallen with America's changing fortunes. A 1949 rally in Augusta, Georgia, attracts a crowd of robed and hooded members.

ious and most vicious hate group in recent history, the Nazis. Nazi ideals caught on not only in Germany but also in other parts of the world. Some hate groups today still carry the Nazi banner.

The Nazis and the Holocaust

Germany at the end of World War I was a badly defeated nation. But the victors in the war, who called themselves the Allies, feared that Germany would raise another army and threaten Europe again. So the Allies demanded that Germany pay for the damage caused by the war. The Allies hoped to prevent another war by leaving Germany without money for arms and ammunition. And, for a time, it worked. So severe was Germany's economic depression after the war that it was unable to pay its debts. The Germans were forced to turn over some of the country's richest regions to France, Poland, Denmark, Belgium, and Lithuania.

The German people seethed with anger about the outcome of the war and their government's inability to improve the country's worsening condition. Feeling helpless, they were ready to follow anyone who would give them a way to fight back. That person was Adolf Hitler.

In 1921, when Hitler took control of the National Socialist party, or Nazi party, it was a small, local political party in the German state of Bavaria. The group was strongly anti-Semitic, or biased against Jews, and anticommunist. They were also nationalistic, showing extreme loyalty to their country. In this atmosphere of bigotry and unease Hitler started his "big lie."

In his book, *Mein Kampf*, Hitler wrote, "The great masses of the people . . . will more easily fall victims to a big lie than to a small one." The lie he told the German people was that they belonged to an ancient Aryan, or white, race that

Adolf Hitler, architect of Germany's genocidal campaign against Europe's Jews, ascends to his place of power at a 1930s Nazi rally.

was superior to non-Aryan races. Non-Aryans included anyone who was not white, along with all Jews, and people with mental and physical handicaps. This message of superiority provided welcome relief for an angry and defeated German public.

Germany, under Hitler and his Nazi followers, waged a war from 1939 to 1945. This war, called World War II, reached across six continents. It claimed 50 million lives. Hundreds of millions were wounded. Countless homes were destroyed and the countryside and cities of Europe and Asia were ravaged.

Though the war was horrible for everyone in its midst, European Jews bore the brunt of

Hitler's viciousness. The Nazi war against the Jews was not a struggle over land and resources. It was not a holy crusade or an attempt to defeat an enemy in order to win a war. The Nazis killed the Jews simply because they were Jews. Hitler and his followers believed the Jews were less than human and sought to wipe them from the face of the earth.

By the end of the war, 6 million Jews had died. The Nazis also murdered at least 250,000 Gypsies, a wandering race of people. Another 5 million non-Jews, considered inferior for one reason or another, also met their deaths in Hitler's concentration camps. Among these were homosexuals, members of certain religious sects such as Jehovah's Witnesses, and persons with physical

The Nazis' system of mass murder was executed with deadly efficiency. To dispose of the bodies—and destroy evidence of the murders taking place—the Nazis burned thousands of corpses in vast crematoriums.

and mental handicaps. This mass extermination of other human beings during World War II is called the Holocaust.

The new Nazis

Although the Nazis were soundly defeated the Nazi ideal of a superior Aryan race still exists today. People who hold this belief are called neo-Nazis, or new Nazis.

In recent years, the neo-Nazi movement has grown in Europe and North America, where troubled economies, high unemployment, and strained resources have heightened tensions. In addition, because of wars or lack of work in their own countries, many people are leaving their

Neo-Nazis gather by the hundreds in Germany in 1991 to commemorate Hitler's campaign of genocide against the Jews.

homelands and are moving to wealthier, more peaceful countries to find work. As Haitians, Hispanics, Middle Easterners, Asians, Indians, Pakistanis, Turks, Yugoslavs, Romanians, and North Africans migrate to the United States, Canada, Britain, Germany, and France, some residents of those countries have begun to feel threatened. Some feel that the immigrants will hurt their chances for jobs in economies that are already weak. Some of these people have turned in fear and anger to the neo-Nazi movement. Those most closely associated with the neo-Nazi movement today are called skinheads.

Skinheads with Nazi views

The skinheads, named for their shaved heads, started banding together in Great Britain in the late 1960s. Many were teenagers from working-class families who had little hope of finding jobs. The economy was weak and there were fewer and fewer jobs for skilled tradespeople.

Skinheads originally became known for harassing and beating up hippies and homosexuals, who led lives different from their own. They also attacked Asians and Pakistanis, immigrants they felt were responsible for the high unemployment rate. They eventually joined the white power movement and added blacks and others to their list of targets.

By the 1980s, the skinheads had spread throughout Western Europe, Scandinavia, Canada, Australia, New Zealand, South Africa, and Latin America. Today there are an estimated eight to ten thousand skinheads in Great Britain; approximately five to ten thousand skinheads in Germany; and about three thousand skinheads in the United States.

The skinheads are not a single organization as is the Ku Klux Klan. Skinheads have formed many groups. While not all skinheads are violent

East German skinheads raise their arms in the Nazi salute at a 1990 demonstration in East Germany.

or even racist, many are both. What most share is a style of dress that includes shaved heads or short-cropped hair and heavy black boots, loyalty to Nazi and white supremacist views, and an appetite for violence against blacks, Asians, gays, and Jews. They are believed to be responsible for much of the violent crime committed by hate groups around the world.

Many skinheads are vocal about their belief in Nazi ideals. They wear or display the swastika, the symbol adopted by Nazis. In public demonstrations they often carry banners that proclaim "Hitler was right," referring to his campaign of genocide, or mass murder, of the Jews. When skinheads gather in groups, many greet each other with the same stiff-armed salute used by Nazis to honor Hitler.

The skinheads are probably the most open about their Nazi views, but other groups share these views. Some of these groups were formed by people who took part in the American Nazi movement of the 1930s and 1940s. Many of these people still hold Nazi beliefs. However, the groups they lead today are joined together by a religion called Christian Identity.

A faith of hate

Wesley Swift, a former Klan organizer from Alabama, founded Christian Identity and his Church of Jesus Christ Christian in the 1960s. The religion is based on Swift's interpretation of the Bible. Swift and his followers believe that whites are the only true children of God. Christian Identity teaches that anyone who is not white is not human and that Jews are the devil's children.

The Christian Identity movement has grown in a climate of wide-scale social change taking place in North America and Europe over the last three decades. Since the 1960s, attitudes toward family, marriage, women in the workplace, homosexuality, and a host of other issues have altered. Divorce has become common. Some couples have chosen to live together rather than marry. Some women have chosen careers over marriage and family while others have chosen all three. Homosexuality is less often the deeply hidden secret it once was and single parenting is gaining in popularity.

Many people feel threatened by these changes. Some who feel threatened have strengthened ties with friends and family, and have renewed their efforts to pass on their own values to their children.

Christian Identity followers have done this, too. However, their religion fails to see the com-

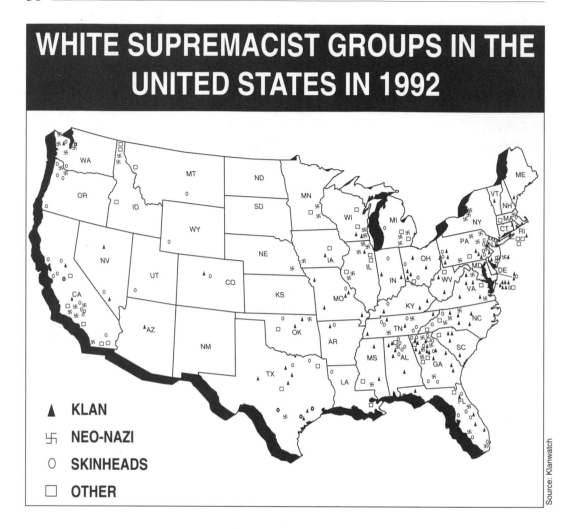

WHITE SUPREMACIST GROUPS IN THE UNITED STATES IN 1992

▲ **KLAN**

卐 **NEO-NAZI**

○ **SKINHEADS**

☐ **OTHER**

Source: Klanwatch

plex processes that bring about social change. Christian Identity teaches that such change is caused by Jews and nonwhites who seek to destroy the white race. This explanation is used to justify the goal of many people in the Christian Identity movement. That goal is elimination of Jews and anyone who is not white, even if this must be done through violence.

Christian Identity is the most influential force in the hate movement today. Dozens of churches teach Swift's narrow view of humanity. Christian Identity also has followers in groups operating outside of the organized Christian Identity churches. One of Christian Identity's strongest supporters is Richard Butler. Butler founded Aryan Nations as a nonreligious branch of Christian Identity. Aryan Nations is headquartered in Hayden Lake, Idaho. The group claims about five hundred members. Its philosophy is simple. "Hate is our law. Revenge is our duty," Butler once told a reporter.

Another group with a large Christian Identity following is Posse Comitatus. Posse Comitatus is Latin for power or force of the county. The group rejects the authority of any government representative or law enforcement agency higher than the local justice of the peace and county sheriff. Members of Posse Comitatus express an extreme distrust of government authority, but especially of the federal government. They believe that Jews

Richard Butler, founder of Aryan Nations, once summed up his views with two simple words: hate and revenge.

and nonwhites control the federal government, run the illegal drug trade, and strive to take away the rights and jobs of whites. They believe that nonwhites and Jews have "polluted Aryan Christian America," said a reporter who interviewed members of the Posse Comitatus.

Aryan Nations and the Posse Comitatus see themselves as defenders of their country and their faith. Some even describe themselves as "Christian patriots," writes author James Aho. They believe the United States is controlled by non-Christian, nonwhite enemies and that they must regain control of the government and destroy those who stand in the way. "There will not be a Jew left in this country when this is over," Posse Comitatus leader and Christian Identity minister Jim Wickstrom has told his followers.

After interviewing more than five hundred Christian Identity followers, James Aho concluded that these "deadly, cold-blooded, serious Christian 'men of integrity' as one described himself . . . [were] retreating to the woods to arm themselves for what they saw as an impending racial war."

An ugly residue

Poor economies, large-scale immigration, and massive changes in society—all the conditions that trigger hate group growth—are present in the world today. And as a result, hate groups are on the rise.

No one really knows exactly how many people belong to hate groups or even how many groups exist. The Southern Poverty Law Center's (SPLC) Klanwatch program, which monitors hate groups, estimates there are twenty-two to twenty-five thousand hate group members in the United States and about 350 organizations. Thousands more people are thought to belong to hate groups outside the United States, primarily in Europe.

Although the hate movement is spreading today, the conditions that trigger hate group growth run in cycles. Hate groups come and go with those cycles. They decline when economic conditions improve, when immigrants merge into a country's mainstream, and when social changes become accepted. However, while they survive, hate groups can have a significant—and often horrifying—effect on individual lives, on state and national governments, and the world. Even after they shrink in size, hate groups can leave an ugly residue of hatred in a society.

2

Inside Hate Groups

HATE GROUP MEMBERS are mostly white, male, and Protestant. Beyond that, they fit no specific pattern. They are almost any age, from under thirteen to over seventy, and hold jobs in a variety of professions and occupations. Educational background also varies; some members are school dropouts while others have advanced college degrees.

Relatively few women belong to hate groups. In general, women are not regarded as capable of being decision makers or leaders in the hate group movement. If they take part at all, they are often expected to take supportive roles. For example, some groups encourage women—usually wives and daughters of members—to form their own branches of the main organization. In some cases, however, women are viewed as untrustworthy, disruptive, and unwelcome. Posse Comitatus, for example, does not allow women to join at all.

An exception may be the skinheads. Klanwatch's Danny Welch says women have taken part in skinhead activities from the start. "Women were in leadership roles from the beginning," says Welch. "They've been out there with their [heavy black boots] from the start, stomping people."

(Opposite page) Two powerful symbols of hatred and intolerance—a cross engulfed in flames and a Klan member in a white, hooded robe—infuse the night with an air of terror.

35

Some hate groups admit women members while others shun them. A rally in Raleigh, North Carolina, brings out female as well as male white supremacists.

People have many different reasons for joining hate groups. Patsy Sims, who interviewed hundreds of Klan members for her book, *The Klan*, suggests that hate groups serve some basic human needs. Those who join the Klan, for example, often have a "need to belong, to feel important . . . to brighten drab lives . . . a need for religious fulfillment, a need to be liked and accepted," reports Sims. Former National Alliance member Tom Martinez expressed similar feelings about his experiences in that organization. Martinez writes: "I had an existence full of meaning . . . for the first time in my life, I had gained respect and with it friends. . . ."

Groups such as these also fulfill other needs for their members. Most do not see themselves as taking part in what is commonly called "the hate movement." Members frequently tell interviewers that they join out of love for their own race rather than out of hatred for someone else's race. "I love my race and regard it as supreme. . . . I do not hate Indians, Orientals, Mexicans or Negroes. . . . I see my race threatened by these races," one hate group member told Idaho sociologist James Aho.

An everpresent fear

The belief that their own race is somehow threatened by people of other races is common. Many members say they see themselves as defenders or protectors of their race, their faith, and their country. They believe all three are threatened by a broad cross-section of their fellow citizens and by changes in lifestyle and values. In response, they seek out others who feel similarly about these issues and then work together to protect what they believe is theirs. "We're not the haters," one group member told Aho. "We're the lovers. We love all that is noble and righteous. We will not stand by and allow the enemies to destroy these things."

The threat and fear of destruction is everpresent in the words and literature of hate groups. Many express a willingness to give their lives for their cause. Said one Christian Identity follower: "I would consider it an honor to kill the enemies of . . . my race, regardless of the price I may pay for the action." Another told Aho: "I am willing to sacrifice everything, even my life, in order that my race might live."

Training for war and possibly that final sacrifice is vigorous. At the twenty-acre Aryan Nations compound in Hayden Lake, Idaho, members routinely train in the use of weapons, guerilla warfare tactics, and wilderness survival techniques. Annual Aryan Nations conferences also feature sessions on creating false identification papers, including driver's licenses and birth certificates, to throw off police in case of arrest. Target practice is a mainstay of annual conferences. Sometimes members shoot at human silhouettes marked with a Star of David, a symbol of the Jewish faith.

Symbols

Symbols are important in many hate groups, but not just as representations of the enemy. Symbols can be used to project an image or message to outsiders or to show unity between members and their cause. For example, most neo-Nazi groups and some other groups display the Nazi swastika symbol. This ancient religious symbol was used by German Nazis to represent Hitler's regime. In the modern world it has come to symbolize Hitler's belief in the superiority of an Aryan race. The swastika also represents the terror and death Hitler brought upon millions of people. Hate group members who wear or display the swastika are, in effect, telling people they share the beliefs of the Nazis.

Skinheads attending an Aryan Nations conference in Hayden Lake, Idaho, give the Nazi salute, a lasting symbol of Hitler's regime.

Another symbol is the burning cross, most closely associated with the Klan. Since the early 1900s, Klan members have used this symbol as a rallying point at their meetings and to intimidate blacks and anyone else who opposes them. Style of dress, and sometimes a uniform, is also a symbol.

The white, hooded robe of the Klan is probably the most well-known hate group uniform. Some groups, such as the White Patriot's Party, wear camouflage combat gear. Although skinheads do not have a uniform as such, many wear heavy boots, jeans, and black jackets, and most shave their heads or wear their hair cropped very short.

In each of these cases the style of dress projects an image. Often the image is one of power

The Nazis adopted as their symbol the swastika, regarded in ancient times as a sign of good luck. Most neo-Nazi groups today still display the swastika as a symbol of their support for Nazi ideals.

A member of the paramilitary Confederate Knights of the Ku Klux Klan takes part in a parade in Raleigh, North Carolina. Some hate group members don camouflage gear as a symbol of their readiness for war.

or intimidation. The combat gear, for example, creates an image of ruggedness and readiness for war. Wearers of skinhead attire often look tough and threatening. The Klan's hooded robes serve a similar purpose. They inspire fear, partly because Klan members usually wore their robes when they carried out lynchings and cross burnings at night. Klan robes also serve a practical purpose: they conceal the identities of their members. This prevents victims from identifying their attackers. It also fulfills a basic need many hate groups and their members have: the need for secrecy.

Secrecy

Some hate groups are quite secretive. Their leaders usually do not reveal member names or membership numbers because they distrust government and other forms of authority. Because some hate group members are involved in crimes and intimidation, the groups often are watched by law enforcement authorities. Group leaders say that by keeping membership information secret, they are protecting members from improper actions by law enforcement officials.

The Posse Comitatus is one example of an organization that maintains strict secrecy. The group is organized into small groups, or cells, of seven members and their families. While members of one cell know each other they do not know who belongs to other cells. The extreme secrecy makes it difficult to know how many people belong to the Posse Comitatus. Estimates vary widely. The Anti-Defamation League of B'nai B'rith (ADL) believes the Posse Comitatus has between 3,000 and 10,000 members. The FBI estimates membership between 12,000 and 50,000. The Posse Comitatus says it has about 100,000 members. Verification of these numbers is nearly impossible.

Secrecy also lends an air of mystery to hate group activities. Mystery can make just about anything more appealing. Writer Charles Dickens believed this to be so when he wrote in 1780, "To surround anything, however monstrous or ridiculous, with an air of mystery, is to invest it with a secret charm, and power of attraction which to the crowd is irresistible."

An aura of mystery

This aura of mystery attracts some members because they feel they are part of a secret, or that they know something other people do not know. That knowledge makes them feel superior to anyone who is not in on the secret. Former National Alliance member Martinez says that Klan training, marches, and meetings gave the group a feeling of fellowship, as if they were "sharing in a great adventure the outside world knows nothing of."

German skinheads resemble skinheads around the world with their short-cropped hair, black jackets, jeans, and heavy black boots.

An Imperial Wizard of the Ku Klux Klan, dressed in the bizarre costume of the Klan's past, awaits the arrival of members at a Klan gathering.

Some groups add to the air of secrecy and mystery by using code words. The Klan, for example, uses passwords such as "Ayak?" meaning "Are you a Klansman?" and "Akia," "A Klansman I am." They also have mystical names for their leaders—a few include Exalted Cyclops, Grand Dragon, Imperial Wizard, Kludd, and Kleagle. A Klan meeting place is known to members as a Klavern.

Although hate groups are usually secretive about their membership and activities, most want to get their message of white supremacy out to the public. Violence once was the chief means of accomplishing this. Although violence remains a way of life for some groups, others have found more acceptable, and often more effective, ways of getting their message out. Some hate groups hand out literature in shopping malls and other public places, while others discuss their views on television talk shows or recruit new members through computer bulletin boards. Politics is also an avenue for making themselves heard. More and more, hate group members are actively and openly backing candidates who share their views. Others are running for public office or making use of ballot initiatives.

Getting the word out

Part of getting the message out to the public includes recruitment of new members. Most people are introduced to hate groups through someone they know, writes James Aho. However, some groups, such as the Ku Klux Klan, Aryan Nations, National Alliance, and White Aryan Resistance, actively recruit outsiders. The groups print, distribute, and sell brochures and leaflets. They sometimes go door-to-door or hand out literature in shopping malls. In addition, hate group members use computerized phone calls to solicit people who might become members, give them support, or give them money.

Sometimes, explains Aho, they seek out people who might be sympathetic to their cause. For example, they might approach groups known for their antigovernment views or for their efforts to impose a particular lifestyle or set of moral values on others. They might also seek out people who are having financial difficulties and who are searching for someone to blame for their troubles.

Although young people do not necessarily fit these categories, they are often targeted for recruitment. In her book *Extremist Groups in America*, Susan Lang writes that the Aryan Youth Movement in California recruits members from punkers, skinheads, and heavy metalists. She

A Klan youth camp, one of many recruitment tools used by hate groups, recruits new members in Alabama.

describes these groups as the Aryan Youth Movement's "most willing audience." Lang also reports that North Carolina's White Patriot's Party formed a branch called the Southern National Front specifically to recruit young people from ages eight to eighteen. Linda Brown, a docent with a traveling exhibit of the Anne Frank Center in Amsterdam, Netherlands, told a group of student visitors that she frequently finds Nazi propaganda lying on the ground at the school bus stop in front of her house. "They want you," she told them. "They think you are too young to understand [what their real goals are], that you are too inexperienced."

Some groups use computer bulletin boards to reach this young audience. A neo-Nazi who runs one such board claims to get twenty-five to thirty calls a day, many from young people. "The major reason for computer bulletin boards is that you're reaching youth—high school, college, and even grade school youth," he says.

To reach the broader public and to influence public policy, some hate groups have turned to politics. In recent years, several political candidates with ties to hate groups have run for public office.

The politics of hate

Tom Metzger, leader of the White Aryan Resistance and former head of the California Ku Klux Klan, believes the time for cross burnings has passed. Politics offers a way to influence public policy. Gaining political and economic power while helping promote other whites, he recently told a newspaper reporter, is the surest way to achieve the goal of an all-Aryan state. "You don't make change having fiery crosses out in cow pastures. You make change by invading the halls of Congress and the Statehouse," Metzger said on another occasion.

Tom Metzger, leader of the White Aryan Resistance, came close to winning a seat in Congress when voters in San Diego, California, chose him as a Democratic nominee. He later lost the election to his Republican opponent.

Metzger is among those who have tried to make their way into the political system. He has run for political office several times. His most successful bid for public office was in 1980, when he won a Democratic congressional primary in San Diego, California. Metzger later lost the election to his Republican opponent.

Louisiana's David Duke, whose résumé includes membership in the American Nazi party and leadership in the Ku Klux Klan, has also run for public office. He won a seat in the Louisiana state legislature in 1989 and ran unsuccessfully for governor of Louisiana in 1991.

David Duke speaks in 1980 as president of the newly formed National Association for the Advancement of White People (NAAWP).

Although Duke lost the governor's race, he attracted many votes—and much attention. Media coverage of Duke's campaign often focused on his Nazi and KKK past and on the organization he founded in 1980, the National Association for the Advancement of White People (NAAWP). Duke describes this group as a "civil rights organization" in the mold of the long-standing civil rights organization called the National Association for the Advancement of Colored People (NAACP). Others call Duke's organization a "Klan without robes."

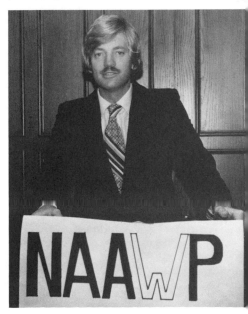

Whichever the case, Duke's comments on the campaign trail made an impact. He beat out a former Louisiana governor in a three-way race and took 39 percent of the vote in the statewide runoff election. Some observers said his polished speaking style and good looks attracted many voters. But others noted that Duke spoke on concerns that have occupied the public in many other elections, including the economy and social reform.

Those who monitor hate groups were not surprised by Duke's strong showing in the election. "If I had to choose anyone from the white supremacy movement to get in a position of power, it would be David Duke," said Danny Welch of Klanwatch. "He used tactics that had never been used before—throw away the robe, put on a three-piece suit, cut your hair, and get yourself on TV."

The 1991 Louisiana governor's race brought David Duke (left) to Louisiana State University in Baton Rouge, where student protestors reminded the public of Duke's Nazi past.

Duke did not express all his views in front of the television cameras, however. In two 1985 newspaper interviews, Duke preached separation between the races in the United States. He also suggested that the Holocaust, during which the Nazis killed 6 million Jews, never occurred. Nor did he mention, as he has in the past, that he considers violence an acceptable way of achieving white supremacy.

Duke once said, "We of the Klan are devoted to political solutions which are constitutional and legal. But . . . we'll fight back any way possible. They have their choice: it'll be ballots or bullets. And if they stop us with the ballot, they're going to get the bullets."

Although some observers were not surprised by Duke's ability to gather votes in the governor's races, others expressed shock at public response to his campaign.

"There is . . . something incredible about Americans voting in large numbers for an admirer of Adolf Hitler," wrote columnist Anthony Lewis in reference to Duke's strong showing. "Less than 50 years ago Americans died fighting the unmitigated [absolute] evil of Nazism. To know that many today would overlook a politician's attachment to that evil . . . is to know something is deeply wrong in this country."

By seeking public office, candidates such as Duke and Metzger have sought to put their groups' beliefs into action. As elected officials, they would be in a position to influence laws and public policy.

Using the initiative process

Citizens who wish to influence public policy without actually running for office have access to other means. Voting is one avenue; when citizens exercise their right to vote they choose the leaders

A Measure 9 supporter urges passage of the initiative in Portland, Oregon. Campaign organizers played on people's fears, much like the Know-Nothings of an earlier era.

who will govern their city, state, and nation. The initiative process is another way for citizens to influence community operations. Initiatives are laws proposed by groups of citizens. If these groups gather the required number of signatures, the proposed law is placed on the ballot and citizens vote for or against the measure. If the proposal passes, the initiative becomes law.

In 1992 a group called the Oregon Citizen's Alliance (OCA) tried unsuccessfully to pass a new law using the initiative process. The law was called Measure 9 on the Oregon state ballot. Opponents said it would have legalized discrimination against homosexuals in Oregon. The law would have required that homosexual behavior be described in the state constitution as "abnormal, wrong, unnatural and perverse." Critics believed Measure 9 would have banned homosexual teachers, allowed landlords to deny housing to homosexuals, and prohibited government-supported AIDS research, counseling, and care.

Members of the OCA do not consider themselves a hate group. However, like the Know-Nothings of an earlier era, the OCA played on people's fears. OCA founder and leader Lon Mabon warned of a "homosexual takeover" of Oregon. Some OCA members claimed that companies in Portland, Oregon, had agreed to hire only homosexuals, although they never offered evidence to support this claim.

The OCA did not advocate violence against homosexuals during the race, but the language of the campaign may have incited some people to commit crimes and violent acts against the measure's opponents. Homosexuals reported an increase in assaults. Cars bearing Measure 9 bumper stickers were vandalized. The offices of the Campaign for a Hate-Free Oregon were burglarized and the names and addresses of supporters stolen. Shortly after the burglary, supporters began receiving anonymous, threatening phone calls. Jim Galluzo, a Catholic priest whose church was burned after he visited homosexual victims of beatings during the 1992 election, told a reporter, "This atmosphere, this feeling of hatred, it's really here."

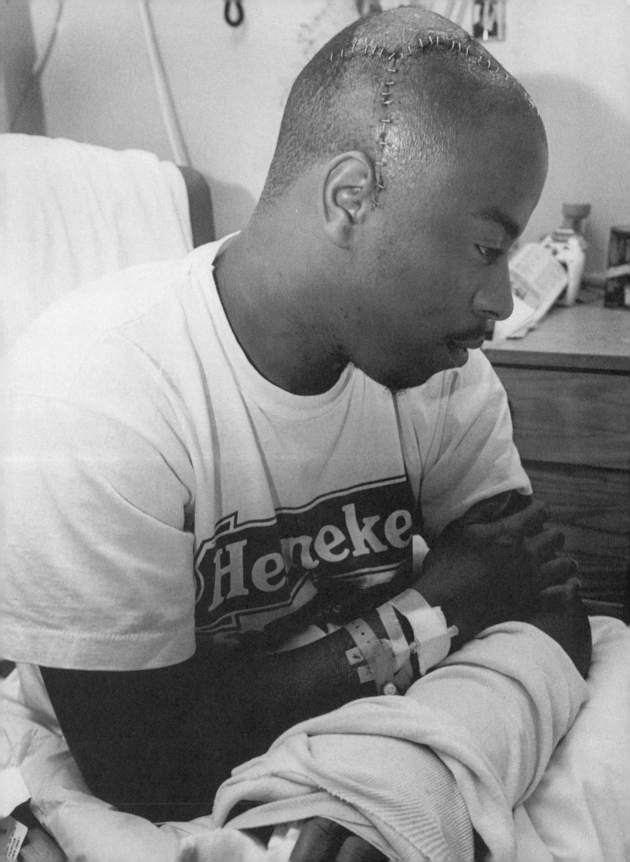

3

Hate Crimes and Violence

HATE-MOTIVATED CRIME and violence is on the rise in the United States and around the world. Some criminal and violent acts are committed by members of organized hate groups, while others are carried out by individuals who are not part of any organized group. Numbers of groups or individuals who have taken part in the violence is unknown. What is known is that the level of hate-motived crime is rising. "All the experts generally agree that hate crimes have reached epidemic levels and that they are still continuing to increase," says Daniel Levitas of the Center for Democratic Renewal, an organization that monitors hate group activity.

Hate or bias crimes include those committed because of the victim's race, religion, ethnic background, gender, or sexual orientation. This means that the person committing the crime has targeted the victim because he or she is black, a Jew, of Vietnamese ancestry, a homosexual man or woman, or any of numerous other traits

Hate crimes and violence take many forms. Some are more serious than others, but all are intended to cause hurt. Vandalism, arson, assault, and murder have all been carried out in the name

(Opposite page) The scars of hate crime and violence run deep, as Tarik Butler can attest. Butler survived a 1992 attack by four white youths who beat him with baseball bats in Staten Island, New York.

51

Vincent Chin was beaten to death by two out-of-work Detroit autoworkers who blamed him for their lost jobs.

of hatred and intolerance. Neo-Nazis in Germany have torn apart Jewish cemeteries and scrawled graffiti on the walls of Holocaust memorials and synagogues. In 1990, three youths constructed a crude wooden cross from chair legs and burned it in the yard of a black family living in Saint Paul, Minnesota. In 1982 in Detroit, Michigan, two out-of-work autoworkers beat Chinese-American Vincent Chin to death. They believed he was Japanese and they blamed the Japanese for the lack of work in Detroit's car industry.

These are but a few examples of crimes and violence of hate. In America alone they number in the thousands, and those who keep track of hate crimes and violence say the numbers are steadily rising. The Southern Poverty Law Center's Klanwatch project has monitored and tallied reports of hate crimes and violence nationwide between 1989 and 1992. Klanwatch figures show that incidents of vandalism increased from 125 in 1989 to 322 in 1992; cross burnings rose from 34 in 1989 to 117 in 1992; and hate-motivated murders increased from 7 in 1989 to 31 in 1992.

Many American cities, counties, and states do not have the resources for tracking hate crimes. But some do and their figures, gathered by a Stanford University Law School visiting scholar, also show increases in hate-motivated crimes and violence. Between 1991 and 1992, hate crimes based on race, national origin, ethnicity, and sexual orientation increased 16.7 percent in a tally of such incidents from selected cities, counties, and states. In New York City, for example, hate crimes rose from 525 in 1991 to 626 in 1992. In Los Angeles County, hate crimes rose from 670 in 1991 to 728 in 1992. The state of Minnesota saw an increase from 425 in 1991 to 433 in 1992, while the state of Florida saw hate crimes climb from 265 in 1991 to 336 in 1992.

Race, according to one FBI report, is the most common motivation for hate crime. Since 1990, federal law has required the FBI to publish annual reports on hate crimes. But many local and state agencies do not submit figures, so the reports are thought to reflect fewer incidents than actually occur. Nevertheless, in 1991 the FBI counted 4,558 hate crimes in the United States. Sixty percent of these were racially motivated, with two-thirds of the crimes committed by whites and almost one-third committed by blacks. The most commonly reported hate crimes were acts of intimidation and property destruction.

Other reports suggest that homosexual men and women are the most common victims of violence. In 1984, a survey of gays and lesbians in eight

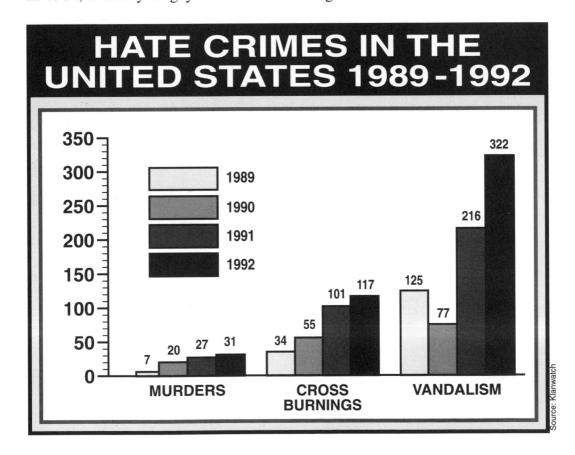

HATE CRIMES IN THE UNITED STATES 1989-1992

Source: Klanwatch

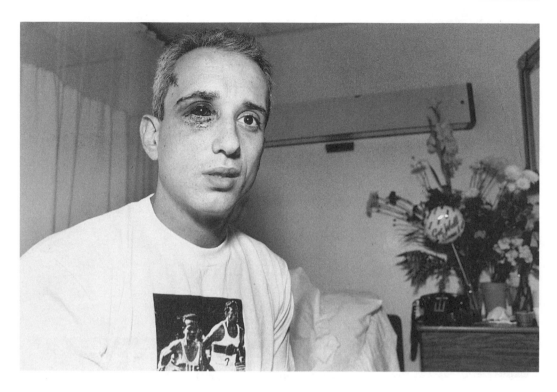

Homosexual men and women are often the victims of hate crimes. Gary Apruzzese was badly beaten while walking with his lover in New York City.

cities showed that 19 percent had been assaulted at least once in their lives because of their sexual orientation; 44 percent had been threatened with violence; and 94 percent had suffered some other kind of abuse, such as random punching, hitting, shoving, or name-calling. The National Gay and Lesbian Task Force Policy Institute reported that in 1986 more than seven thousand incidents of intolerance of gays were recorded. Homosexuals are "by far the most frequent victims of hate crimes," writes Jan Phillips of the American Civil Liberties Union (ACLU) in Kentucky.

A long history

Hate group involvement in crime and violence has been well documented over many decades. During the civil rights era of the 1950s and 1960s the Ku Klux Klan "took law and order and morals into its own hands, and flogged and lynched and tarred and feathered and fed screaming victims through rock grinders. Live cremations were sometimes staged before spellbound audiences in town squares and parks," writes Patsy Sims. Between 1954 and 1965, according to the U.S. Justice Department and local police, the Klan was involved in almost seventy bombings in Georgia and Alabama, the burning of thirty churches in Mississippi, the "sadistic castration" of a black man in Alabama, twelve murders in Alabama, three murders in Mississippi, and a shooting in Georgia.

"The most violent group"

Today, skinheads and other neo-Nazi groups seem to have taken up where the Klan left off. One Klanwatch report describes skinheads as "the most violent group of white supremacists this country has seen in a quarter century." In the United States, author Susan Lang writes that skinheads have been responsible for approximately fifteen hundred unprovoked attacks against Jews, African-Americans, Hispanics, Asians, and homosexuals.

Further evidence of skinhead involvement in violence surfaced in July 1993 when police officers in Los Angeles, California, arrested members of a group called the Fourth Reich Skinheads. Law enforcement authorities say members of the group were plotting to start a race war. They planned to start this war in Los Angeles, authorities said, by killing Rodney G. King, the man at the center of a highly publicized police brutality case; by blowing up the First African Methodist Episcopal Church, the city's oldest black church; and by attacking prominent African-American and Jewish leaders.

The arrests followed an eighteen-month investigation by the FBI and other law enforcement

Federal and California officials display high-powered assault weapons, a Confederate flag, and a photograph of Adolf Hitler confiscated during July 1993 raids on a band of white supremacists.

agencies. Investigators described the Fourth Reich Skinheads as a band of young white supremacists with ties to the White Aryan Resistance and the Church of the Creator, both well-known white power groups. The Fourth Reich Skinheads are thought to have between eighteen and fifty members, many of whom are under age thirty.

Skinheads in Europe have also been at the center of violent attacks, mostly on immigrants. In Czechoslovakia skinheads have assaulted Turks, Arabs, Vietnamese, and Gypsies. Before East and West Germany reunited as one country in 1990, East German skinheads were responsible for approximately two hundred hate-motivated attacks a year. Since reunification, German neo-Nazi skinheads have hurled stones and firebombs at hostels where foreign guest workers live and have attacked Poles crossing the German-Polish border.

In one horrifying attack on October 2, 1991, three teenage skinheads threw a firebomb into the home of a Lebanese family living in the town of Huexne. The bedroom in which Fauzi and Zubeida Saado's six children slept burst into flames. Two of their daughters, Zeinab, age eight, and Mokadas, age five, were badly burned. Zeinab barely survived the attack.

Adding to the horror of that night was the scene outside the Saado home, as Fauzi Saado screamed for help. His German neighbors, drawn out of their own homes by the sound of the explosion, did not offer help. "Nobody called the

Firebomb in hand, a German neo-Nazi youth takes part in rioting in front of a hostel which houses foreign workers and immigrants.

Members of Aryan Nations pass out literature. Few hate groups openly encourage violence but sometimes the literature they distribute incites violence.

police. Nobody came to help us. They just kept their distance and watched. Nobody came to help! People were just running away," Fauzi and Zubeida told the *Los Angeles Times.*

Not all hate groups take part in violence of this sort. In some cases, where violence occurs, it is carried out by individual members acting on their own rather than on instructions from the group or its leaders.

Few hate group leaders openly encourage members to commit violence. However, the writings and speeches of some leaders can incite criminal or violent behavior. For example, the leader of the National Alliance, William Pierce, has written a novel called *The Turner Diaries.* Although it is a work of fiction, some groups have used the book as a manual for the white power movement. The book suggests that thousands of people should be murdered to purify the white race. This includes Jews, people of color, white women who have had relationships with men of color, and anyone working for the state, local, or federal government, including teachers, lawyers, judges, police, and politicians. Pierce also discusses sabotage of dams and power plants as a means of gaining power over the government.

The Turner Diaries inspired the founding of the Order, an ultra-secretive group of about forty members. The Order, which is thought to have disbanded after FBI arrests in the 1980s, was dedicated to achieving the goal of racial purity described in Pierce's book, says former Order member Tom Martinez. Toward that end, Order members planned to blow up dams and power stations in the Pacific Northwest. The resulting chaos, they believed, would create a political crisis during which they could seize power. The plan was foiled when Martinez was arrested. Pressure from his family and fears for his own safety prompted Martinez to turn against the group and become an informer for the FBI.

Order members have been linked to other violent and criminal acts, including the murders of Denver radio talk-show host Alan Berg, an Order member suspected of violating the group's secrecy oath, and a Missouri state police officer.

Weapons stockpiles

Law enforcement authorities have captured or learned of huge stockpiles of weapons held by hate group members. Posse Comitatus members, for example, are usually "armed to the teeth," writes author James Ridgeway. When one Posse Comitatus stronghold in Nebraska was raided by federal officials in 1985, they found thirty semi-

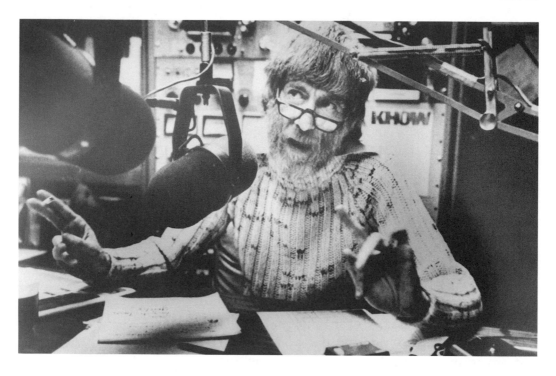

Members of the white supremacist group The Order have been linked to the murder of Denver radio talk-show host Alan Berg. Berg was shot to death in 1984.

automatic and assault rifles, thirteen automatic pistols and rifles, and 150,000 rounds of ammunition. They also discovered a bunker stocked with food and water and Christian Identity literature.

In another FBI raid, this one on the 224-acre compound of The Covenant, the Sword and the Arm of the Lord in Arkansas, federal agents discovered grenades, mines, ammunition, gallons of cyanide, a tank, and a bomb-making factory.

A former member of the White Patriot's Party also testified that the North Carolina group had bought plastic explosives, blasting caps, night-vision scopes, grenades, dynamite, antitank rockets, and surface-to-air rockets stolen from military bases in the state.

Hate groups or their members are not solely responsible for hate crime. Many hate crimes are committed by individuals with no connection to any hate group. Many of these crimes are also committed by individuals with no criminal history. "Most perpetrators of crimes of prejudice are . . . our neighbors and our neighbors' children," writes Joan Weiss, director of the National Institute Against Prejudice and Violence.

Racist motives

Racism is frequently the motive for these random acts of crime and violence, as it was in the case of Johnny McCool. McCool, a young black man of nineteen, was assaulted in July 1989 as he made a call from a phone booth in Glendale, California, a mostly white area. Ralph Tavlian, a white man who owned a garage near the phone booth, grabbed McCool, began slapping him, and yelled, "Nigger, you don't belong in this city. We don't need people like you here."

In this case, the assault was committed by a lone individual. Hate crime is usually carried out by a group of attackers pouncing on a lone victim. Often the attackers are armed while the victim is not.

Nineteen-year-old Luyen Phan Nguyen, an immigrant from Vietnam, was the victim of a group attack at a party in Florida in 1992. When party goers began hassling him and calling him names, Nguyen tried to leave. Nguyen was chased down and beaten to death by seven to fifteen white men as dozens of people watched. "This incident represents a degree of racial savagery we haven't seen in 10 years," said Dennis Hayashi, cofounder of the National Network Against Anti-Asian Violence.

Those who track hate crimes in the United States have noticed another disturbing trend. Young people commit many of the random bias attacks in the United States. In 1990, there were twenty hate-motivated murders in the United States. More than half were committed by people under twenty-one; in five cases, both the criminals and the victims were under twenty-one.

Reports from at least two states support these findings. In 1991, ten juveniles under age ten were charged with hate crimes in New Jersey. Another 173 hate crimes were committed by young people between the ages of eleven and seventeen. In New York City, the New York Police Department reports that 50 percent of all bias crimes are committed by people under nineteen. In some cases, assaults by young people outnumber the attacks by organized hate groups. "We are finding out that it is juveniles and not organized hate groups who are responsible for most of the bias crime in New Jersey," says state attorney general Robert Del Tufo.

Victims of hate

People who commit hate crimes believe that their actions prove their strength and superiority. Through their actions, they hope to drive minori-

A group of Belleville, Michigan, high school students gives an ugly demonstration of intolerance.

ties out of an area, off a job, or away from a school. In extreme cases, they may want to eliminate the group they hate completely.

Sometimes their actions achieve their goals. Often, they do not. But hate crimes almost always destroy the victims' peace of mind and sense of community belonging. Hate crimes invade the privacy of homes and places of worship. One interracial couple was harassed for three years. Says their son, "My mom used to walk and talk to people. Now she's afraid. She just sits inside and reads all the time."

Hate crimes sometimes inspire their own legacy of fear, bitterness, anger, frustration, and hate. Crime victims may grow to hate the groups of people to which their tormentors belong. For example, one concentration camp survivor, who lost his entire family during the Nazi Holocaust, cannot bear to be around Germans. He says, "I know it's wrong, but I can't stop the hate."

Young victims of hate crimes are particularly affected, as they have difficulty coping with the

Teenagers in Chicago flaunt their racist message and jeer participants of a civil rights march.

Hundreds of mourners attend a 1955 funeral service for Emmett Till, a fourteen-year-old black youth murdered while visiting relatives in Mississippi.

strong emotions. Two young victims, a fourteen-year-old boy and his sister—both black—were attacked in 1992 in New York City by four white men who screamed racial insults at them and smeared them with white paint. The boy told a reporter, "I feel a certain way about white people right now. I don't want to feel this way, but that's how I feel: angry, angry that this had to happen and that I have to change my school because I don't want to go back. . . . The way black people and white people feel about each other—it has to stop."

The victim and the victim's family rarely avoid this legacy of anger and hate. However, when victims refuse to hate the person who harmed them, they break the chain of hatred. In 1955, Mamie Mobley's fourteen-year-old son, Emmett Till, was viciously murdered while visiting relatives in Mississippi. Till was black; his killers were white. One of Till's killers said he had killed the youth because he had spoken to a white woman. When a reporter asked the mother what she would do to her son's murderers if she had the chance, she said:

> I would do nothing. . . . It was not for me to go around hugging hate to myself because hate would destroy me. It wouldn't hurt them. . . . I did not wish them dead. I did not wish them in jail. . . . I haven't spent one night hating those people. I have not looked at a white person and saw an enemy. I look at people and I see people.

Hate crimes and violence are the most vicious actions of prejudiced individuals or of hate groups. However, hateful words, degrading nicknames, and racial insults also cause pain and anguish. Hateful words attack a person's sense of self-worth, and often dehumanize individuals.

Because of the mental pain and damage that hateful words can cause, some people think hateful speech should be outlawed. They think that this would increase respect for people of different races, religions, ethnic backgrounds, and sexual orientation. Increased respect, they reason, might result in fewer hate crimes. There are others, however, who believe that restricting speech, whether hateful or not, violates the First Amendment to the U.S. Constitution.

4

Freedom of Speech and the Messages of Hate

(Opposite page) Police in riot gear patrol the area around a Ku Klux Klan rally in Atlanta, Georgia, in an effort to prevent violence between opposing groups of demonstrators. As offensive as their views might be, hate group members—like other Americans—are free to publicly express their beliefs.

"CONGRESS SHALL MAKE no law . . . abridging the freedom of speech . . . ," reads part of the First Amendment to the U.S. Constitution. Freedom of speech is the right to say or write or publish one's thoughts, or to express one's self. This right is guaranteed to *all* Americans. But does this include all forms of expression, even those that are ugly or hurtful? And who decides this complicated issue?

The U.S. Supreme Court interprets the Constitution and determines whether particular kinds of expression are protected by the First Amendment. The Supreme Court justices have decided that some kinds of speech are not protected by the Constitution, meaning a person does not have a constitutional right to make certain comments. For example, neither libel nor slander (written and verbal speech that damages someone's reputation) are protected by law. A newspaper may not write that a business executive is stealing money from a company if the newspaper knows this to be untrue, for example. False advertising

67

and obscenities (sexually explicit material which lacks "serious literacy, artistic, political or scientific value") are not protected either. The justices have also decided that "fighting words," or "conduct that itself inflicts injury or tends to incite immediate violence," should not be protected under the First Amendment. This includes abusive, personal insults that are likely to cause a violent reaction in an ordinary person.

Unlike fighting words, hate speech has traditionally been protected under the Constitution. This has caused much confusion since the difference between fighting words and hate speech is not always clear. Hate speech has been described as words and actions that intimidate, threaten, or encourage harm. Most often these words and actions are directed at a person because of his or her religion, race, ethnic background, or sexual orientation. One writer has gone so far as to call hate speech a "hate-driven threat of assault." At the very least, hateful words may hurt someone's feelings, attack self-esteem, or create fear.

Viewed in this light it is difficult to understand why hate speech is protected by the Constitution. Yet that is the position of the U.S. Supreme Court, which has repeatedly ruled that Americans must be free to express themselves even when the views expressed are hateful or hurtful. This protection also extends to hate groups. Though their words might offend, they too have a right under the Constitution to express their opinions and beliefs. And, this they do in a variety of ways.

Spreading the message of hate

Traditionally, hate groups have printed pamphlets and flyers and handed them out. They have made speeches to gatherings of members. Today they reach larger audiences through electronic media. For example, in Colorado, Utah, Idaho,

Tom Metzger interviews a white supremacist leader on his television show, "Race and Reason."

and California, Christian Identity groups own and operate radio stations which they use to broadcast messages of white power.

Groups also use television to air their views. The Federal Cable Act of 1984 requires local cable stations to provide free public access to citizens, without exercising any "editorial control over content." Under this law, White Aryan Resistance leader Tom Metzger was able to produce and air a talk show called "Race and Reason." On the show, Metzger asks guests about their views on race and politics and their activities against nonwhites and Jews. Metzger also sponsors a telephone "hate line," which members and non-members can call for Metzger's latest recorded message. One such message states:

> We will create a revolution in this country. We will put the blood on the streets like you've never seen. And advocate more violence than both world wars put together. . . . We have a new set of targets to play with. . . . If you're white and work for the system, watch your step. . . . Next time you run across a white cop, a white judge, or a white lawyer, don't hesitate to act. A fight to the death and nothing less.

Some hate groups use computer bulletin boards to carry their messages of hate. One bulletin board has displayed the names and addresses of members of organizations that monitor hate group activity and messages that often contain thinly veiled threats. For example, Glenn Miller, a former member of the Klan who formed the White Patriot's Party, has told members of his group: "We have an up-to-date list of many of the Jew headquarters around the country so that you can pay them a friendly visit." Miller does not openly threaten anyone with this message. However, his group is devoted to overthrowing the U.S. government and killing blacks and Jews.

The Skokie march

The First Amendment not only protects verbal expressions of feelings and opinion. It also protects actions that express feeling and opinion. For example, the display of symbols, flag burning, marches, parades, and demonstrations are all considered forms of expression and are protected under the Constitution. This protection has been challenged at various times.

This happened in 1978 when a group of Nazis planned to march in the Chicago suburb of Skokie, Illinois. Skokie's population is 60 percent Jewish—approximately seven thousand residents are survivors of Nazi concentration camps. Hundreds of articles in magazines and newspapers discussed the proposed march.

The Nazis claimed the march was intended to be peaceful. Many others, however, did not see it that way. In the *National Review*, writer Hadley Arkes claimed that the march was "a deliberate attempt to provoke a population to violence." A *National Review* editorial said, "[The march] is intended to insult the dead, to celebrate their mur-

Supreme Court rulings have held that flag burning is a form of political expression protected by the First Amendment to the U.S. Constitution.

derers, and to convey a threat, however impotent, against the living."

The city of Skokie tried to stop the march by passing ordinances that required the group to provide $350,000 in insurance, prohibited the wearing of military-style uniforms, and prohibited the distribution of hate literature. As hateful as the Nazi group's views might be, especially in a community with so many Jewish concentration camp survivors, the American Civil Liberties Union (ACLU) felt these ordinances violated the marchers' right to free speech. The ACLU felt that if the Nazis' right to free expression was curbed or taken away, the free speech rights of others could also be removed. The ACLU acted on behalf of the Nazis in this case because "the danger to the First Amendment . . . was too great for us to stand by silently," an ACLU lawyer said. The ACLU action reflected the view that the First Amendment allows people to exchange ideas freely and honestly, even when those ideas are offensive to others.

A federal judge ruled in 1978 that the American Nazi party had a right to march in the heavily Jewish community of Skokie, Illinois.

A mock slave auction at the University of Wisconsin in Madison in 1988 sparked protests from students offended by the racist nature of the event. Events such as this have led to speech codes and other restrictions on university campuses around the country.

The lower courts did not uphold efforts to keep the Nazis from marching in Skokie. But the march was later moved to Chicago because of threats of violence.

A speech code

Although the courts have traditionally protected actions and speech that express opinion, even when the views expressed are hateful, this protection is increasingly being questioned. Lawyers, civil rights leaders, government and university officials, and others have tried to create rules and laws that would curb hate speech without violating the Constitution.

One university that tried to address the problem of hate speech was the University of Wisconsin at Madison. Several times in the late 1980s, the largely white student body held degrading events. For example, the students held a "Martin

Luther Coon" picnic on the birthday of Martin Luther King Jr. "Coon" is an offensive term used by some people in reference to a black person. Racial tensions grew as black students reported harassment by white students. A white student told a black student, "You're taking up the place of a smarter white student because of quotas. . . . We don't want your kind here."

University administrators were split over whether to devise a campus hate speech code that would protect minority students from harassment and intimidation. Some felt such a code was badly needed, that students should be able to pursue their studies in peace. Others worried that a speech code would create an atmosphere in which free speech was discouraged. Erroll B. Davis Jr., a university regent, argued that insults and demeaning words were indeed harmful and that students should be protected from them. Davis, a black man and chief executive officer of Wisconsin Power & Light, explained his belief that there is no such thing as perfectly free speech. He explained that certain kinds of speech that hurt, insulted, frightened, or endangered others were already restricted and that he could not understand why hate speech should be treated differently. Davis told reporters:

> The crux of the issue is whether you accept that words wound. That "sticks and stones" routine is a crock. You have to draw the line when behavior affects others. We have free speech as much as we have pure milk. You can't go to the airport and joke about bombs. . . . It's labeled sexual harassment if my son whispers lascivious [indecent] comments to your daughter behind the counter at work. But if you whisper racist epithets [insults] to my son in front of the counter, it's exalted speech meriting constitutional protection.

In the end, university administrators passed a code that prohibited "racist or discriminatory

Robert Viktora placed a burning cross in the yard of a black family living in Saint Paul, Minnesota.

comments, epithets [abusive words or phrases], or other expressive behavior" which deliberately demeaned or intimidated others.

Almost immediately administrators found themselves investigating all kinds of charges. Most had nothing to do with hate speech. One man was upset about being called a "primitive dinosaur," for example. Administrators found out how difficult it could be to enforce the hate speech code. In addition, people were beginning to question whether the code was constitutional under the First Amendment. Because of some of these problems, university administrators drafted and enacted a new code in 1992.

However, a June 1992 Supreme Court ruling on another case put the university's speech code on hold. That case grew out of a cross burning in Saint Paul, Minnesota.

The burning cross of Saint Paul

In 1989, in response to a growing number of hate crimes in Saint Paul, Minnesota, the city council passed a hate crime ordinance. The ordinance read, in part, "Whoever places on . . . private property a symbol . . . including but not limited to a burning cross or Nazi swastika, which . . . arouses anger, alarm or resentment in others on the basis of race, color, creed, religion or gender commits disorderly conduct and shall be guilty of a misdemeanor."

This law was tested one night in June of 1990, when three youths built a crude cross out of broken chair legs, climbed over Russ and Laura Joneses' fence, and burned the cross in the Joneses' yard. The Joneses were the first black family to move into their working-class neighborhood in Saint Paul. In the first three months of residence, their car tires were slashed, their car window was broken, and their five children were called names.

Seventeen-year-old Robert Viktora was arrested in connection with the cross burning and charged with vandalism, trespassing, and the threat of violence. He was also charged with violating Saint Paul's hate crime ordinance. In fighting the charges, Viktora's attorney argued that the hate crime ordinance violated his client's right to free expression guaranteed under the First Amendment. The case made its way through the lower courts and all the way up to the U.S. Supreme Court.

In June 1992, the Court ruled that the Saint Paul law was unconstitutional. Essentially, the justices said that Saint Paul could not pass a law

Russ and Laura Jones and their children. The Saint Paul family found Viktora's burning cross in their yard. The cross-burning, and the Supreme Court decision that followed, sparked a nationwide debate about the meaning of free speech.

against language or "expressive conduct" (such as cross burning) simply because the city did not like the message—that of bias against those of a different race, religion, ethnic background, or sexual orientation—conveyed by the language or the conduct.

Free speech or personal attacks?

The Court also addressed a problem that the University of Wisconsin had already encountered: that many people considered any insult to be hate speech. Saint Paul's ordinance covered only insults, or "fighting words," directed at someone because of race, color, creed, religion, or gender. The Supreme Court justices wrote that, in order to be fair and protect all citizens, Saint Paul should have covered all fighting words in its ordinance, including those that "express hostility, for example, on the basis of political affiliation, union membership, or homosexuality." In other words, remarks about "thieving Democrats," or "dumb Teamsters" would have to be prohibited as well as those such as "dirty spic," which is a derogatory term for someone of Hispanic descent. The justices said that to interpret the term "fighting words" so broadly would make people afraid to say anything about anyone and, in the end, would stop all free speech. Such a law would be almost impossible to enforce, too, as the University of Wisconsin discovered when it tried to enforce its hate-speech code.

In arguing the issue, however, four justices disagreed with the majority opinion. Justice Harry A. Blackmun said there was a difference between speech that does not harm someone and speech that does. He explained that insulting a person's political party or union was not a personal insult, because it could not result in someone feeling frightened or bad about themselves. However, in-

Supreme Court justice Harry A. Blackmun recently wrote that First Amendment protections would not be compromised by limits on personal insults and intimidation.

sulting or intimidating a person because of his or her race, religion, ethnic background, gender, or sexual orientation had immediate harmful consequences.

Justice Blackmun also said he did not agree that preventing hateful speech in the form of vandalism and intimidation would limit the free speech rights of American citizens. "I see no First Amendment values that are compromised by a law that prohibits hoodlums from driving minorities out of their homes by burning crosses on their lawns."

Justice Byron R. White wrote that the Court's decision seemed to tell the public that protecting hate speech was more important than protecting the people threatened by it. However, he said, "expressions of violence, such as the message of intimidation and racial hatred conveyed by burning a cross on someone's lawn" were not more important than protecting the public. That is why "fighting words" had been considered outside of First Amendment protection.

Justice White wrote that he feared the decision appeared to say that hate speech and intimidation were acceptable ways of expressing one's opinion. The decision, he wrote, "legitimates hate speech as a form of public discussion."

Many people were unhappy about the Supreme Court's decision in the Saint Paul case. "It seemed like they [the justices] ignored the entire fact that hate crimes exist and people should be protected from them," said Steven Zachary, president of the Saint Paul chapter of the National Association for the Advancement of Colored People (NAACP).

Laura Jones, on whose lawn the cross was burned, said that her children (the oldest was eleven at the time of the incident) had been forced to face racism as a reality in their lives. "It

Justice Byron R. White worries that a recent Supreme Court decision leaves the impression that hate speech and intimidation are acceptable forms of expression.

makes me angry that they have to be aware of racism around them, that they notice it more and more. They're too young for that. They're just children. That's one reason why I'm so disappointed with the decision."

The impact of the Supreme Court decision

U.S. Supreme Court decisions affect all laws. State and local laws and ordinances that are similar to those challenged in the Court must conform with the Court's decisions. Court rulings such as the 1992 decision on the Saint Paul cross burning can also indicate to state and local lawmakers which of their other laws might be open to a Supreme Court challenge.

Many state and local governments have laws and ordinances against hate crimes. These include acts such as vandalizing a synagogue with swastikas or cross burnings. However, the Supreme Court's decision in the Saint Paul case broadly defined the right to free speech to include the right to hate speech and expressive actions such as cross burnings. That meant that, if challenged in the Supreme Court, the laws against hate crimes in many states could also be found unconstitutional.

As a result of the 1992 Saint Paul case, forty-six state and numerous local governments have been reviewing or repealing their hate-crime laws. They want to avoid having their laws challenged in the Supreme Court. As many as one hundred colleges and universities, including the University of Wisconsin, had implemented rules against bias-motivated speech and actions. They, too, have begun to reverse their stands to avoid legal challenges.

However, many state officials feel there is a pressing need for a curb on the language and actions that may lead to hate crimes. As a result, thirty-one attorney generals across the country have joined with civil rights groups to ask the Supreme Court to reconsider its decision.

Some people, however, do not want to wait for the Supreme Court to make hate speech and hate crimes officially unacceptable. They want to stop hatred, bigotry, and the groups these attitudes spawn. And they want to do it now.

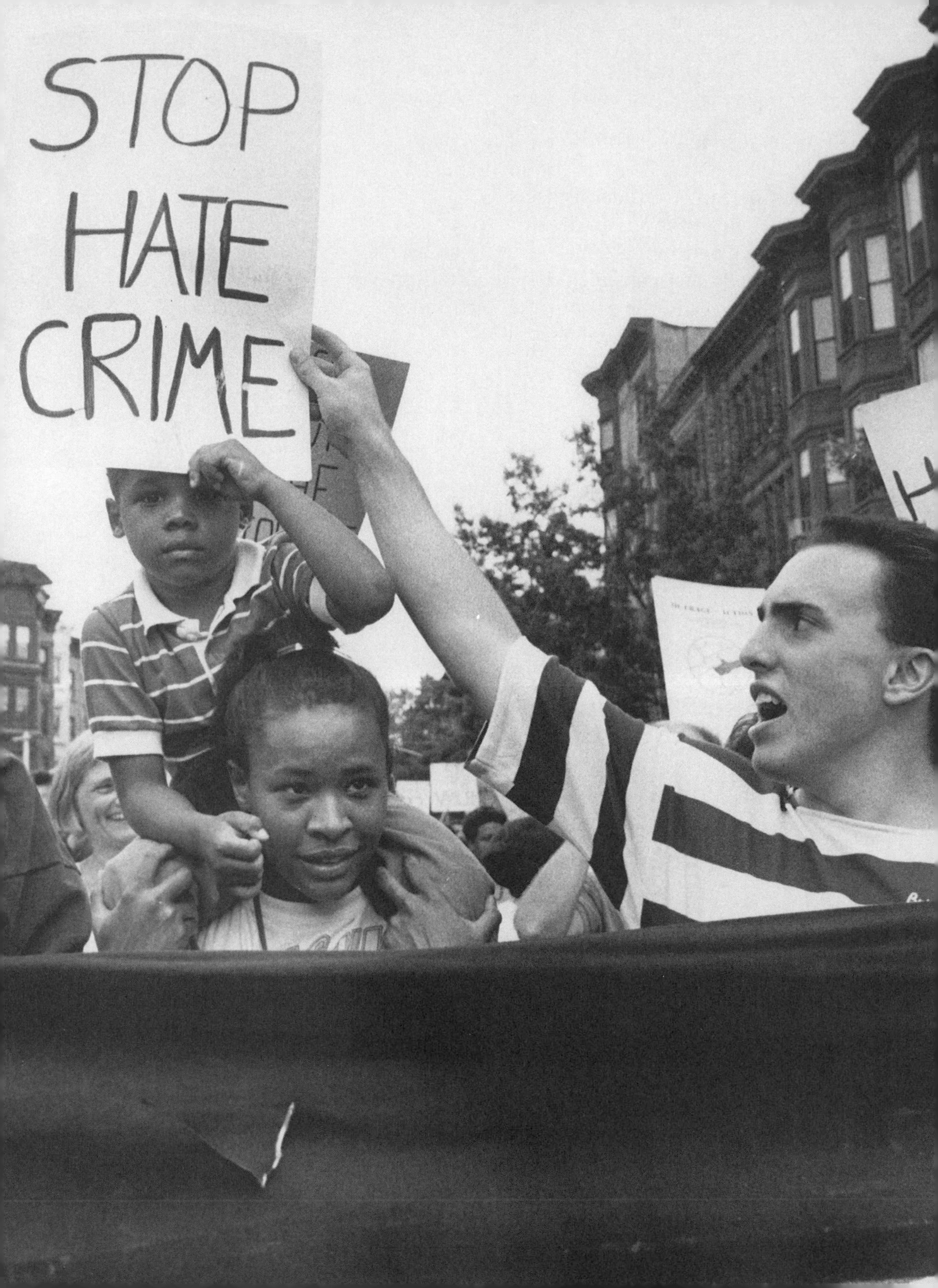
STOP
HATE
CRIME

5

Turning Off
the Hate

HATE GROUPS GROW during times of uncertainty, change, and fear. However, chances are they would not exist at all if more people learned to know and tolerate others. So one key to eliminating hate groups is the campaign against ignorance and intolerance. This can be done through education both in schools and in the community. Young and old alike must learn to accept and appreciate the differences in people if hatred is to disappear.

Communities must also send a clear message to hate groups that their behavior will not be tolerated. This message is sent by community and government leaders, police, and ordinary citizens through the laws they make, vote for, and enforce.

Turning off the hate is not an easy or an overnight process. It requires a great deal of work by many people. A 1990 Klanwatch report describes the task of eliminating hate this way:

> For legislators, it means drafting·laws to address the threat of hate crime. For educators, it means finding ways to open the channels of cultural understanding among children. For police, it means increased attention to acts of hate violence. For

(Opposite page) Residents of Brooklyn, New York, demonstrate their resolve to halt hate crimes and bias-motivated violence in their neighborhoods.

neighborhoods, it means strengthening the bonds of community to embrace diversity and reject bigotry. And for every individual, it means seeking understanding in place of resentment and of desiring peace in the place of conflict.

Today, committed people are using all these means to combat hate groups.

Hate groups and the law

One weapon used in the battle against hate groups is the legal system. For years, law enforcement agencies lumped hate crimes together with other crimes. They did not separate an ordinary arson, for example, from one motivated by bias. For that reason, no one really knew how many hate crimes were occurring. So before officials could address the problem of hate crimes and hate groups, they first had to determine how

Law enforcement agencies are stepping up efforts to punish hate crimes such as those that drove Dudley Emmons and his family from their Chicago home. The garage was burned, an awning torn down, a brick thrown through the living room window, Emmons's car window smashed, and his family verbally harassed.

large the problem really was. Congress took a step toward this end in 1990. They passed the Federal Hate Crimes Statistics Act, which requires the Justice Department to gather data on bias crimes from sixteen thousand police department across the country.

The Justice Department is also stepping up the prosecution of racist, skinhead, and anti-Semitic groups who commit bias crimes. In 1989 the Justice Department prosecuted forty-two people on charges related to hate-motivated cross burning, vandalism, arson, and shooting. "This aggressive prosecution . . . should serve notice to youthful racists as well as those who inspire them, that hate crimes simply will not be tolerated in a free society," wrote *Common Cause* magazine.

On the local level, many police departments have set up hate crime units that aggressively pursue those who commit bias crimes. For example, in 1991 undercover police agents in Houston went into a neighborhood noted for attacks on homosexuals. Three officers were attacked almost immediately: two with mace and one with a baseball bat. Police arrested thirteen people, including five juveniles who were harassing gay pedestrians. Predicting that other police departments would follow Houston's lead, FBI representative Harper Wilson told reporters, "This kind of operation—targeting these attackers—may be unusual now, but it will not be unusual for long."

The hate factor

In many states, those who are convicted of hate crimes face stiffer sentences than they would have faced for the same crime without the hate factor. The state of Wisconsin, for example, permits prosecutors to seek higher penalties for criminals who "intentionally select" their victims "because of their race, religion, color, disability, sexual orientation, national origin, or ancestry."

This law was put to the test in 1989 in Kenosha, Wisconsin. A group of black teenagers, angry about a scene in the movie *Mississippi Burning*, in which a white man beats a black youth, were urged by one member of the group to attack a fourteen-year-old white boy. The boy was beaten unconscious and suffered permanent brain damage.

The ringleader, Todd Mitchell, was convicted and sentenced to four years in prison instead of the two-year sentence he would normally have been given for the crime. His attorneys argued that he should have been charged only for the crime, not the motivation behind it. Others said that the law allows for harsher punishments when a victim is "intentionally selected," such as when a police officer or the president of the United States is killed. So harsher punishment should also be permitted when hate crime victims are intentionally selected because of their race, religion, ethnic background, gender, or sexual orientation.

This case went before the U.S. Supreme Court after numerous appeals in the lower courts. In June 1993, the Supreme Court ruled that courts could enhance or extend the sentences of those found guilty of hate crimes.

Criminal laws affect only those who commit crimes. Those who might encourage a crime, but do not actually take part, usually go unpunished. This concerns some civil rights attorneys who believe that sometimes a hate group leader or the whole group should also take responsibility for the criminal actions of members. Specifically, when a leader's comments or a group's philosophy or literature incites violence or crime, that

leader or group should also be punished, some civil rights lawyers say. Lawyers have turned to the civil lawsuit to address this issue.

The price of hatred

A civil lawsuit is an action between two private parties, one of whom feels wronged. If the wronged person wins the suit, the court can order the losing side to pay money for damages to the winner.

Civil lawsuits can be brought against hate groups and hate group leaders even if they were not directly involved in or charged with a crime. The object of the lawsuit is to wipe out the hate group's money supply. If the group is ordered to pay large amounts of money to victims of hate crimes, attorneys hope that the group will not have enough money left to run their organization. In that way, the lawsuit curbs the group's activities.

Civil rights attorneys have asked the courts to punish hate groups and their leaders when the group's literature or philosophy incites crime or violence.

The first time a hate group was sued for its role in a murder was in 1984. The murder that prompted the lawsuit occurred in 1981 in Mobile, Alabama. It involved members of the United Klans of America (UKA). UKA members were angered by the outcome of a trial in which a black man was accused of killing a white police officer. The accused man said he had killed the officer in self-defense. After hearing both sides of the case, the jury was unable to reach a verdict.

Members of the UKA seethed over the hung jury. As they saw it, a black man had gotten away with murdering a white man. They decided to take matters into their own hands. According to later testimony in court one of the UKA members said, "There ought to be a damned nigger hung." Three of the men set out to do just that.

Their victim was nineteen-year-old Michael Donald. Donald had no connection to the murder case. He was chosen simply because he was alone and black. Three of the Klansmen kidnapped him at gunpoint as he walked to a local store. They drove him to a secluded area, beat him unconscious with a tree limb, strangled him, cut his throat, and then hung him from a tree. One of the men convicted in Donald's killing said that the purpose of the murder was "to show the strength of the Klan . . . to show that they were still here in Alabama."

Punishing those who urge violence

On the strength of this remark, Southern Poverty Law Center attorney Morris Dees sued the UKA group. To win, Dees had to prove that the Klansmen had conspired, or planned together in advance, to kill someone, and that in doing so they were acting on behalf of the Klan. Dees said later: "I suspected Shelton [Robert Shelton, UKA Imperial Wizard] and the UKA officials knew

Nineteen-year-old Michael Donald—kidnapped at gunpoint, beaten, and his throat cut— hangs from a tree limb, a reminder for all time of the gruesome reality of racial hatred.

As editor and publisher of the UKA publication The Fiery Cross, *Robert Shelton (right) was found to have encouraged violence against blacks.*

from past experience that UKA members resorted to violence in carrying out UKA's goals, and that they encouraged it."

Dees was able to prove that several of the men involved in planning the Donald killing, as well as two involved in the actual murder, were Klan officials. He proved that the UKA had a history of violence going back almost twenty years. And he was able to show that Shelton, as editor and publisher of the UKA's official publication, *The Fiery Cross*, encouraged violence. One issue of the newspaper contained a drawing of a black person who had been lynched. The caption read, "It's terrible the way blacks are being treated. All whites should work to give blacks what they deserve."

As a result, the court ordered the UKA to pay Beulah Mae Donald, the murdered young man's mother, $7 million in damages. As partial payment, the UKA was forced to turn over their headquarters building, which was valued at $250,000.

This decision was important because it showed that hate groups could be held accountable for the criminal actions of their members. Dees used the same strategy in 1990 to win a $12.5 million judgment against Tom Metzger and his son John of the White Aryan Resistance (WAR). In 1988, Metzger had sent his son to Portland, Oregon, to recruit skinheads for WAR. While there, Dees contended, John Metzger encouraged the skinheads to engage in racial violence. Dees said Metzger had urged the skinheads to attack Jews and blacks with baseball bats.

The night of Metzger's visit, three skinheads beat Ethiopian student Mulugeta Seraw to death with baseball bats. Dees was able to prove that the Metzgers and WAR had incited the violence that led to Seraw's death. Dees won his case. The Metzgers were ordered to give up their home, several bank accounts, 25 percent of their earn-

Tom Metzger (left) and his son John prepare to leave a news conference in Oregon after losing a civil lawsuit which linked them to the beating death of an Ethiopian student.

ings, and any contributions that come in to WAR to satisfy the judgment against them.

"The reason we asked for so much, and the reason the jury gave it to us, is the signal it would send to the organized hate business," said Dees after the trial.

Legal approaches to fighting hate groups can only be used after a crime has been committed, property has been damaged or destroyed, or someone has been threatened, hurt, or killed. By the time a conviction or decision is made on a case, a community has often been torn apart. Lawsuits and the sentencing of criminals do little to help heal communities, redirect hate group members, or protect potential victims of hate crimes. Community action, however, can accomplish all of these.

Southern Poverty Law Center attorney Morris Dees has successfully used civil lawsuits to punish and cripple hate groups whose members commit crimes.

Communities discourage hate groups

"The greatest allies hate groups have in a community are fear and silence, and the greatest enemy is simple, unequivocal, public rejection," according to the Southern Poverty Law Center. Communities around the world are rejecting hate groups in a variety of ways. They are forming community watch programs, sponsoring educational programs, making media and local government representatives aware of problems in their area, and holding demonstrations.

In 1992 in Newburgh, New York, for example, three weeks after a one hundred-member Klan rally in their town, three thousand residents demonstrated against the white supremacist group. "Hate and racism won't survive—can't survive—in a community that has finally come alive," said Newburgh mayor Audrey Carey. "Let us make a definitive and strong statement to those hatemongers—they will not, will not, will not be tolerated in this community."

A march against racism in Washington, D.C., provides concerned citizens with a chance to clearly state their views.

Residents of Contra Costa County, California, also responded strongly when the Ku Klux Klan tried to make its mark in their mostly white community in the early 1980s. The Klan had harassed black families by starting fights, breaking windows, and shooting up and burning homes. The sheriff's office and county officials were slow to respond and even denied that there was a problem in the county. So a small group organized a community meeting to discuss the situation. They expected fifty to seventy-five people at the meeting; almost five hundred residents showed up.

The group, which came to be called the Coalition Against Racist Violence (CARV), took the protection of the harassed families into their own hands. They posted twenty-four-hour volunteer watches at victims' homes to monitor police response to the harassment, and they confronted anyone who tried to harass the families. This eventually stopped the attacks. The media focused attention on the group's efforts, forcing county officials and the sheriff's office to begin investigating the harassment.

The coalition established a hot line for victims to report crimes. Then they arranged a hearing with the California Department of Fair Employment and Housing (FEH), which monitors discrimination complaints. They managed to involve the state legislature and local congressional representation. And they kept up their media campaign.

Two years of effort brought results. The group saw substantial changes in their community. Anti-racism classes started in the schools and teachers received training in race relations. Civil lawsuits were brought against the sheriff's office for failing to protect the victims of hate crimes. The first minority representative in the county's history was elected to the school board. Although there are still incidents of racism in the county, the community now has a way of helping residents handle hate crimes. Contra Costa County residents have clearly rejected the Klan.

Giving German skinheads a place of their own

Communities in the United States are not the only ones devising ways to cope with hate groups. When neo-Nazi skinheads, in Mölln, Germany, hurled Molotov cocktails into an apartment house in November 1992, the German government and public responded. The apartment housed Turkish guest workers, many of whom had lived in Germany for a generation. A woman, age fifty-one, and two little girls, ages ten and fourteen, were killed. Nine others were injured, including a nine-month-old baby.

The German government and police in several cities arrested dozens of neo-Nazis and seized

Faruk Arslan mourns the deaths of his mother, daughter, and niece, who were killed in November 1992 when neo-Nazi skinheads hurled Molotov cocktails into their apartment. The poster behind him reads: "Children murderer, pigs, neo-Nazis."

their weapons. But the most impressive response came from the German public. More than 1 million Germans took to the streets to show their support for the foreigners in their country. In Munich, 400,000 people held a candlelight vigil on city streets. Celebrities made televised public-service announcements opposing racial and ethnic hatred.

Some German cities have tried more controversial approaches. The German government is providing funding to develop social clubs for neo-Nazi skinheads. They hope that giving the skinheads a place to go will keep the young people off the streets and out of trouble. The clubs provide the skinheads with their own gym and disco and allow the youths to hang racist banners and posters that express their views. "We're trying not to shut out these kids. There's a tendency to say they're lost causes. But we can't just shove them aside," says Barbara Graf of Frankfurt's International Association of Social Workers and Youth Workers. The program sponsors hope that by showing the young people they are accepted members of society, the youthful Nazis will give up the group on their own.

A wise solution?

Many people question the wisdom of these kinds of clubs. They see the clubs as governmental encouragement of Nazi philosophy. "You can't rule out the possibility that having their own club will make them more political," says Reinhard Herwig, police chief in Görlitz. Although sympathetic to the young people's confusion, he's wary of creating another Nazi era. "These kids have no right to go running around giving the Hitler salute in the street because they have no idea what Hitler's fascism wrought on the world."

Germans turn out by the thousands to protest skinhead violence in their towns.

Program sponsors, however, are aware of the risk. They are ready to shut down the clubs if they find that the program is strengthening the neo-Nazi movement. "If we find that the club has become a Nazi nest, they're out overnight," says Joachim Richter, city council chairperson for the Youth Assistance Committee.

As mentioned, program supporters hope that by giving young skinheads a form of acceptance, the youths will voluntarily reject their hate-filled and violent philosophy. There is some reason to hope this strategy will succeed, for some hate group members have renounced their bigotry and broken the cycle of hatred. Families and friends can often influence a hate group member's decision to break away.

A change of heart

One hate group member who eventually gave up his message of intolerance was Greg Withrow. In 1979, Withrow founded a group of white supremacists, the White Student Union, at American River College in Sacramento, California. For seven years he was a vocal advocate of white power. At the Aryan Nations conference in 1986, for example, Withrow told the crowd, "Men, women, and children without exception, without appeals, who are of non-Aryan blood shall be terminated or expelled [from the country]."

The following year, however, Withrow met a woman who convinced him to renounce his racist stance. Soon afterward, he appeared on a television talk show where he criticized white supremacists and announced that he was writing a book about his former group's activities. Not long after the show aired, his former friends broke into his apartment, beat him with a baseball bat, and stole the manuscript. Later that summer they waylaid him in the street, beat him, gagged him, nailed him to a board, cut his throat, and left him.

Miraculously, Withrow regained consciousness and, still nailed to the board, staggered into the street looking for help. The first three people he met—all white—turned away from him, but a black couple coming out of a night club stopped to help him. This act of kindness left a big impression on Withrow. Says Withrow now:

> I want people to see that this is what I get because this is what I created. What goes around, comes

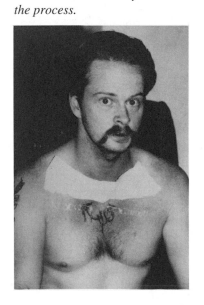

Greg Withrow, founder of the white supremacist White Student Union, gave up his hate group involvement and nearly died in the process.

around. I've said a lot of terrible things and I've spread a lot of harm. I don't want to hate anymore. I don't want to hurt anymore.

Individuals and the end of bigotry

Getting to know and respect people as individuals is the strongest weapon against hate groups and the best prevention of the crimes they commit. If one knows a person and his or her problems, it is hard to treat the person as something to be feared and, as a result, hated.

Students may have a particularly hard time breaking the cycle of hate. They are often under pressure to go along with the opinions of their peers, to laugh at ethnic jokes, or to use racial slurs. Docent Linda Brown tells students who visit the traveling "Anne Frank in the World" exhibit that these comments and jokes turn people into objects.

> When you turn people into objects and give everyone the same characteristics, you are doing just what Hitler did. You're starting the process again. Let others [who tell such jokes] know that you don't look at people as objects, but as people. When you stand up for people as individuals, you break the cycle.

It also takes courageous adults to break the cycle. For example, in the 1970s C.P. Ellis was a Klan leader in Durham, North Carolina. He was in constant conflict with one of the town's leading black activists, Ann Atwater. "I hated [her] with a purple passion," said Ellis. He felt that Atwater's habit of speaking out and organizing demonstration was responsible for some of the growing integration of Durham. However, he changed his mind about Atwater when the two of them served together on a local school committee.

At first, neither Ellis nor Atwater was happy about the idea of working together. But neither wanted to be seen as a coward, afraid to deal with his or her opponent. And both wanted to do something about their children's education. So each agreed to the appointment.

The first meetings were difficult, recalled Atwater. "When I first met C.P. Ellis, he didn't want anything to do with niggers. I would always say, 'Well, I don't want anything to do with crackers.' We kept it up . . . cussing each other back, we couldn't get anything done."

It was not long, however, before they discovered that their similarities were greater than their differences. Both were criticized and rejected by people in their respective races for their work on the committee. Blacks were stunned that Atwater would work with a Klan member. Whites accused Ellis of "selling out," of opening the door to more

The strongest weapon against bigotry and hatred is getting to know and respect people as individuals.

school integration. Both had children in school who were being taunted by schoolmates because of their parents' work on the committee. In addition, both were poor and undereducated and felt that their poverty and lack of education made them less respected in the community. Said Ellis:

> I begin to see, here we are, two people from the far ends of the fence, havin' identical problems, except her bein' black and me bein' white. From that moment on, I tell ya, that gal and I worked together good. I begin to love the girl, really. Up to that point, we didn't know each other. We didn't know we had things in common.

Ellis gave up the Klan and his prejudices. He eventually came to accept black people as individuals and was in turn accepted by the black community. Members of the black community came to trust Ellis to such an extent that he was elected chief steward and business agent for his union, which had a 70 percent black membership, by a vote of 134 to 41.

The school committee experience opened Atwater's eyes as well. "There's been a change in me like the change in C.P. I used not to talk to any white people, now I talk to any of them. . . . At the end, C.P. and I could lock hands and say we won."

Taking a stand

The benefits of taking a stand against hatred are many: reduced crime, improved personal and community relations, and the development of a healthy community. Because communities are made up of individuals, it is up to individuals to take a stand against hatred. When one does, one automatically sets an example to others, perhaps giving them courage to take a stand also.

When no one sets an example, however, hatred and fear can take over. Too often, people close their eyes to the actions of hate groups because of apathy or fear. People may be indifferent to hate groups because they are not the groups' targets. In Nazi Germany, for example, many non-Jews turned their backs on the persecution of the Jews because they were not affected directly. Pastor Martin Niemöller, a president of the World Council of Churches, opposed Hitler and as a result spent several years in concentration camps. Historians say Niemöller issued this warning to later generations who might ignore hatred because they think it does not concern them:

> In Germany they came first for the Communists, and I didn't speak up because I wasn't a Communist. Then they came for the Jews, and I didn't speak up because I wasn't a Jew. Then they came for the trade unionists, and I didn't speak up because I wasn't a trade unionist. They they came for the Catholics and I didn't speak up because I was a Protestant. Then they came for me, and by that time there was no one left to speak up.

Fear, too, often prevents people from opposing the actions of hate groups. Some people are afraid that if they speak out, the hate group will turn its anger on them. Attorneys such as Morris Dees have found that witnesses may be reluctant to testify against groups such as the Klan because they fear physical attacks. But people can fear other kinds of attacks as well. In the 1920s, people in the Midwest often failed to stand up against the Klan because they feared political or economic reprisals.

In 1924, for example, William E. Wilson, an Indiana Democratic representative to the House of Representatives, ran for a second term. The Klan tried to force him to join "or *else.*" When he refused, they started a smear campaign that cost him the election. At the time, Wilson told his son:

> We've gone a long way in this country, but apparently still haven't freed men and women of their suspicion of each other, their prejudices, their in-

Pastor Martin Niemöller, who opposed Hitler and spent several years in concentration camps because of his actions, warned the world against ignoring hatred.

tolerances. I think that this is going to be the big battle of this century.

Wilson was right. Almost seventy years later, Americans and others around the world are still fighting that battle. Former Massachusetts senator Birch Bayh, now chairman of the National Institute Against Prejudice and Violence, says that everyone must take a stand against those

> who espouse prejudice and bigotry and who, if left uncontested, will divide and destroy our nation. Let each of us now stand up and speak out against those purveyors of hate and prejudice . . . traitors to the American cause. Let us tear off their hoods, eradicate their brotherhoods, and leave them naked in the light of day.

Hands raised in solidarity, a crowd of thousands symbolizes the potential for harmony between people of different races, religions, and ethnic backgrounds.

Organizations to Contact

The following organizations provide services or information about hate groups and hate crimes. They also offer information that can be used for increasing understanding between people of different races, religions, and ethnic backgrounds.

American-Arab Anti-Discrimination Committee
4201 Connecticut Ave. NW, Suite 500
Washington, DC 20008
(202) 244-2990

The committee collects and disseminates statistics on anti-Arab hate crime. The group also works to remove defamatory or insulting stereotypes from media such as films and videos. It also offers a variety of publications about the stereotyping of Arabs in the media, a newsletter, and a hate crime statistic report. Local chapters provide speakers for community groups.

The American Friends of the Anne Frank Center
106 E. 19th St., Fourth Floor
New York, NY 10003
(212) 529-9532

The center is committed to defending democracy and human rights. It does this primarily through education, by developing materials for use in the classroom and sponsoring exhibits such as "Anne Frank in the World: 1929-1945."

American Jewish Committee
Institute of Human Relations
165 E. 56th St.
New York, NY 10022
(212) 751-4000

The thirty-two chapter American Jewish Committee offers a wide variety of surveys on how different groups of people feel about each other. It has also developed a variety of programs designed to educate the community. The group is best known for its project called "Hands Across the Campus," a program that teaches young people about hatred and stereotyping.

Anti-Defamation League of B'nai B'rith (ADL)
823 United Nations Plaza
New York, NY 10017
(212) 490-2525

The ADL monitors and exposes hate groups and their activities. The group works to counteract the influence of hate groups through education and by working with state and national governments to develop hate crime laws. ADL issues various reports on hate group activities.

Center for Democratic Renewal
PO Box 50469
Atlanta, GA 30302
(404) 221-0025

The Center for Democratic Renewal was started in 1979 as the National Anti-Klan Network. It is a coalition of religious, civil rights, and community groups that monitors the activities of hate groups and helps communities fight hate violence. The group offers many different publications, including the handbook *When Hate Groups Come to Town.*

Klanwatch Project
Southern Poverty Law Center (SPLC)
400 Washington Ave.
Montgomery, AL 36104
(205) 264-0286

Founded by the SPLC in 1980, Klanwatch monitors hate crimes and the activities of white supremacists. The group works to stop the actions and violence of hate groups through educational programs such as their *Teaching Tolerance* program for schools. The group's parent organization, Southern Poverty Law Center, engages in lawsuits against hate groups. Klanwatch offers various publications.

Suggestions for Further Reading

Janet Bode, *Different Worlds: Interracial and Cross-Cultural Dating*. New York: Franklin Watts, 1989.

Irene Bennett Brown, *Morning Glory Afternoon*. New York: Atheneum, 1981.

Morris Dees, with Steve Fiffer, *A Season for Justice: The Life and Times of Civil Rights Lawyer Morris Dees.* New York: Charles Scribner's Sons, 1991.

Anne Frank, *Anne Frank: The Diary of a Young Girl*. Garden City, NY: Doubleday and Company, Inc., 1967.

David Gelman, "Why We All Love to Hate," *Newsweek*, August 28, 1989.

Susan S. Lang, *Extremist Groups in America*. New York: Franklin Watts, 1990.

Thomas Martinez, with John Guinther, *Brotherhood of Murder*. New York: McGraw-Hill, 1988.

Works Consulted

ADL Special Report, *Neo-Nazi Skinheads: A 1990 Status Report*. Anti-Defamation League of B'nai B'rith, 1990.

James A. Aho, *Politics of Righteousness: Idaho Christian Patriotism*. Seattle, WA: A Samuel and Althea Stroum Book, University of Washington Press, 1990.

"All Things Considered," "Neo-Nazis in America," National Public Radio, Washington, DC, 1985.

Peter Applebome, "Duke: The Ex-Nazi Who Would Be Governor," *The New York Times*, November 10, 1991.

Laurent Belsie, "The Face of Hatred in America," *The Christian Science Monitor*, November 27, 1991.

Laurent Belsie, "What Is a Hate Crime?" *The Christian Science Monitor*, November 27, 1991.

Cristina Bodinger-de Uriarte and Anthony R. Sancho, *Hate Crime: Sourcebook for Schools*. Los Alamitos, CA: Southwest Center for Educational Equity, Southwest Regional Laboratory; and Philadelphia: Research for Better Schools, 1992.

David Freed, Michael Connelly, and Sonia Nazario, "Southland Is Ripe Turf for White Hate Groups," *Los Angeles Times*, July 7, 1993.

Linda Greenhouse, "The Court's 2 Visions of Free Speech," *The New York Times*, June 24, 1992.

Linda Greenhouse, "The Supreme Court: High Court Voids Law Singling Out Crimes of Hatred," *The New York Times*, June 23, 1992.

Marshall Ingwerson, "Free Speech Under Review in Minnesota Cross Burning Case," *The Christian Science Monitor*, December 4, 1991.

Tamara Jones, "Loads of Fun for Neo-Nazis," *Los Angeles*

Times, June 15, 1992.

Elinor Langer, "The American Neo-Nazi Movement Today," *The Nation*, July 16 and 23, 1990.

Maria Newman, "Victim of Bias Attack, 14, Wrestles with His Anger," *The New York Times*, January 9, 1992.

The New York Times, "Excerpts from the Supreme Court's Decision on Speech and Crimes of Bias," June 23, 1992.

James Ridgeway, *Blood in the Face: The Ku Klux Klan, Aryan Nations, Nazi Skinheads, and the Rise of a New White Culture*. New York: Thunder's Mouth Press, 1990.

Arthur M. Schlesinger Jr., "From Factions to Parties," *History of U.S. Political Parties, Volume I: 1789-1860*. New York: Chelsea House Publishers with R.R. Bowker Company, 1973.

Michelangelo Signorile, "Behind the Hate in Oregon," *The New York Times*, September 3, 1992.

Patsy Sims, *The Klan*. New York: Stein and Day, 1978.

Robert E. Sullivan, "Oregon Postcard: Bashers," *The New Republic*, September 21, 1992.

Robert E. Sullivan, "Postcard from Oregon: Revolution Number 9," *The New Yorker*, November 9, 1992.

Studs Terkel, *Race: How Blacks and Whites Think and Feel About the American Obsession*. New York: The New Press, 1992.

Richard K. Tucker, *The Dragon and the Cross*. Hamden, CT: Archon Books, 1991.

U.S. Commission on Civil Rights, "Bigotry and Violence on American College Campuses," October 1990.

David van Biema, "When White Makes Right," *Time*, August 9, 1993.

Joan C. Weiss, "Prejudice, Conflict, and Ethnoviolence: A National Dilemma," *USA Today*, May 1989.

Randall Williams and Lyn Wells, eds., *When Hate Groups Come to Town: A Handbook of Model Community Responses*. Atlanta, GA: Center for Democratic Renewal, 1986.

Helen Zia, "Women in Hate Groups," *Ms.*, March/April 1991.

Index

About the Author

Sharon Elaine Thompson is a freelance writer. She has written on a variety of subjects, including jewelry and gemstones, copper mining, singing sand dunes, wildlife, and people. In her quest for stories, she has visited the Namib Desert in Africa and the gem-mining areas of Brazil. She has authored two other books: one on the greenhouse effect and one on the La Brea tar pits.

Thompson has lived in the United States and Japan. She now lives in Oregon.

Blairsville High School Library

Picture Credits

Cover photo © Jim McNee 1990/FPG

Adolf Hitler: Bilder aus dem Leben des Fuhrers, Hamburg: Herausgegeben Vom Cigaretten, 1936/Simon Wiesenthal Center Archives, Los Angeles, CA, 24

AP/Wide World Photos, 38, 60, 64, 69, 82, 88, 89, 94, 98

The Bettmann Archive, 16, 42

Donna Binder/Impact Visuals, 48, 80

Culver Pictures, Inc., 12, 20

Robert Fox/Impact Visuals, 99

Jerome Friar/Impact Visuals, 36, 40

Historical Pictures/Stock Montage, Inc., 15

© 1990 Lynn Johnson/Black Star, 74, 75

Library of Congress, 14

Andrew Lichtenstein/Impact Visuals, 46, 50

T.L. Litt/Impact Visuals, 90

National Archives, 25

© Eric Pasquier/SYGMA, 86

Rick Reinhard/Impact Visuals, 90

Reuters/Bettmann, 10, 26, 28, 41, 56, 57, 92, 93

Loren Santow/Impact Visuals, 8, 63

© Tony Savino/SYGMA, 58

© Steve Schapiro/Gamma-Liaison, 96

© Randy Taylor/SYGMA, 85

University of Wisconsin-Madison News Service, 72

UPI/Bettmann Newsphotos, 18, 19, 21, 22, 31, 34, 39, 43, 45 (both), 52, 66, 70, 71, 76, 77, 87

Jim West/Impact Visuals, 62